ADVANCE PRAISE

"Neil Francis has faced neurological adversity with remarkable courage, and come through on the other side. His optimism and positive attitude, combined with great determination, shine through every page of *Positive Thinking*, which is a fine testament to his inspirational approach to overcoming cognitive deficits."

Robert McCrum, Associate Editor of the *Observer* and author of *My Year Off: Rediscovering Life After a Stroke* (Picador)

"This is a fascinating book!

"Neil blends solid research and his own inspiring story to inject every page with hope, positivity and possibility. Few books are game changers – this one may well be. I will certainly be recommending *Positive Thinking* to my business book club!"

Jill Garrett, Executive coach, consultant and former European Managing Director of the Gallup Organization

"In a world that spins faster than ever before, it's easy to become a spectator of our own lives: wondering what to do, struggling to find the time, feeling overwhelmed. This pithy, punchy, personal journey digs into the psychology of positivity and will help you find your passion and purpose."

Professor Andrew Sharman, International consultant and author of *The Wellbeing Book*

"Always engaging and accessible, this book both challenged and reaffirmed aspects of my own journey as a social entrepreneur. It also offered practical advice, based on Neil's ideas and thoughts about positive thinking, for the road that still lies ahead."

Chris Wilkins, Co-founder at Sporting Memories Network

"Neil's moving story, insights and advice make this book an enjoyable and engaging read. It's a valuable tool for anyone who is interested in personal development and achieving their full potential."

Sally Bibb, Author of *The Strengths Book* and Founder of Engaging Minds

"Neil Francis manages to weave his personal experiences with existing ideas on positive thinking and well-being in an engaging text. Drawing on contemporary examples and practical advice, he offers an opportunity to use positive thinking to capitalize on the possibilities that present themselves while recognizing our own capabilities."

David Marshall, Professor of Marketing
and Consumer Behaviour,
University of Edinburgh Business School

"Neil weaves together experiences from his business life, his wide-ranging reading and thinking, and inspirational life stories from famous names and personal acquaintances. But what really draws you into this unique book is his honesty and openness about his personal journey following a life-changing stroke and how it has shaped his own positive thinking. The result is an accessible, empathetic, and down-to-earth read which left me feeling good about the world – which was the whole point!"

Tim Walsh, Professor of Critical Care at
the University of Edinburgh and Consultant
in Critical Care, NHS Lothian

Published by
LID Publishing Limited
The Record Hall, Studio 204,
16-16a Baldwins Gardens,
London EC1N 7RJ, UK

info@lidpublishing.com
www.lidpublishing.com

A member of:

BPR
Business Publishers Roundtable

www.businesspublishersroundtable.com

© Neil Francis, 2019
© LID Publishing Limited, 2019

Printed in Latvia by Jelgavas Tipogrāfij
ISBN: 978-1-912555-15-4

Cover and page design: Caroline Li

THINKING

HOW TO CREATE A WORLD

NEIL FRANCIS

MADRID | MEXICO CITY | LONDON
NEW YORK | BUENOS AIRES
BOGOTA | SHANGHAI | NEW DELHI

In memory of Becca Henderson.
A remarkable, brave and inspirational young woman.

TO START, A STORY
TO GET YOU IN
THE RIGHT MOOD
FOR MY BOOK

In a village on the coast of Mexico, an American businessman was standing on the pier when a small boat with just one fisherman docked. Inside his boat were several large yellowfin tunas.

The American complimented the fisherman on the quality of his fish and asked him how long it took to catch them.

"Only a little while," the Mexican fisherman replied.

The American then asked the man why he didn't stay out longer and catch more fish. The Mexican said that he caught enough to meet his family's needs.

"But what do you do with the rest of your time?" the American asked.

"I sleep late, fish a little, play with my children, take a siesta with my wife, Maria. Each evening I stroll into the village, where I sip wine and play guitar with my amigos. I have a full and busy life, señor."

The American scoffed at this: "I'm a Harvard MBA and I could help you," he said. "You should spend more time fishing, and with the proceeds, buy a bigger boat. With the proceeds from the bigger boat, you could buy several boats. Eventually, you'd have a fleet of fishing boats, and instead of selling your catch to a middleman you'd sell it directly to the processor.

"Then you could open your own cannery. You'd control the product, processing and distribution. You'd need to leave this small fishing village and move to Mexico City, then on to Los Angeles, and, eventually, to New York City, where you'd run your expanding enterprise."

"But señor, how long would all this take?" the fisherman asked.

"Fifteen, maybe twenty years," the American replied.

"But what then, señor?"

The American laughed and said: "That's the best part. When the time is right, you would announce an IPO and sell your company stock to the public. You'd become very rich. You'd make millions!"

"Then what, señor?"

"Then you'd retire. Move to a small fishing village on the coast, where you'd sleep late, fish a little, play with your grandchildren, take a siesta with your wife. In the evening you could stroll to the village, sip wine and play guitar with your amigos."

CONTENTS

ACKNOWLEDGMENTS

Well, this is book three and, as ever, I have had so many people helping me.

So, massive thanks go to:

Fiona Maciver and Helen McGillivray, who read the first draft of the manuscript.

Steve Dalgleish, Becca Henderson, Kari Spence and Rachel Woods for allowing me to share their remarkable stories.

My long-suffering GPs, Dr Claire Doldon and Dr Gabriele Salucci! Dr David Gillespie, my neuropsychologist, and all the brilliant doctors, nurses and speech therapists in the NHS who have helped me in so many ways to recover from my stroke.

The fantastic team at LID Publishing, especially Sara Taheri, Martin Liu, Caroline Li, Susan Furber and Sue Littleford.

As always, my daft golden retrievers – Dougal and Archie – whose walks on the beaches of North Berwick gave me the perfect space to think and plan the book.

Jack, Lucy and Sam, who helped motivated me with their encouragement and love.

Finally, and most importantly, my lovely wife Louise, whose help and support made this book become a reality.

INTRODUCTION

MY
STROKE OF
DISCOVERY

Let's start with a statement that might surprise you.

Having a significant stroke at age 41 turned out to be one of the most positive things that has ever happened to me.

Now, this might be a very strange thing to admit, and I can only say it 13 years on from my stroke. But it really has. It has opened up so many possibilities that I can honestly say would not have occurred if I had not had the stroke.

But on 20 October 1996, when I was lying in the stroke ward of the hospital, unable to speak, with my memory in shreds and temporary blinded in my right eye, it was the worst thing that had ever happened to my family and me. For well over three years it was a very difficult and challenging time for everyone.

So how, you might ask, have I concluded that an event that was horrific initially has now become such a good thing in my life? This event and subsequent challenges have led me to finally understand the power of positive thinking and how to use it in my life. But this is a different type of positive thinking for the 21st century. And used in the right way, I have found it has created many new possibilities in my life. In this book, I am going to share what this type of positive thinking consists of.

Common positive thinking philosophies that have permeated Western society for the last 75 years claim that mere visualization is the key to succeeding and achieving anything that you want. And that the only things that stop you from achieving happiness, good health and wealth are your negative thoughts – and to succeed you must block or ignore them. This book will provide a different, better and more realistic understanding of positive thinking. But, before I describe the type of positive thinking that I am advocating, it will help to explore where the idea of thinking only positive thoughts and blanking out negative ones comes from, and why some of its core tenets are flawed.

THE POSITIVE
THINKING MOVEMENT

In 1937, Napoleon Hill published *Think and Grow Rich*, a book that has reportedly sold over 15 million copies to date. One of the key lessons from this book is that the material universe is governed quite directly by our thoughts. By simply visualizing what you want out of life and thinking positive thoughts, those things and more will be delivered to you – especially if those things involve money. The past few decades have been a profitable era for all sorts of self-help and business success books. Napoleon Hill blazed a trail for an entire industry.

In 1952, Norman Vincent Peale published his book, *The Power of Positive Thinking*. His core argument is that by using the power of focus and believing in success you will overcome any obstacles in your life. No matter how insurmountable it may seem, there is no problem in your life that cannot be overcome by the power of positive thinking.

More recently, in 2006, Rhonda Byrne's book, *The Secret*, suggested that you have the ability to be whatever you want to be. And that if you send out good thoughts and intentions to the universe, the universe will give you good things in return. She says positive thoughts attract happiness and, conversely, negative thoughts attract bad decisions and fuel existing worries and negativity. Byrne claims that focused concentration combined with positive thinking will lead to happiness and wealth.

These three authors, and many others, subscribe to basically the same thing – think positive things, visualize the success that will make you happy and wealthy, and you will achieve anything you want.

Now, there is some merit in this type of 'positive thinking' and millions of people have benefited from some of this teaching. For example, in 1960, Napoleon Hill and W. Clement Stone published *Success Through a Positive Mental Attitude*, where they promoted the same idea as Peale. They coined the term 'positive mental attitude' (PMA). Today, there is a lot of scientific evidence from well-respected psychologists and scientists that having a positive mental attitude can provide a wide range of health and emotional benefits.

However, the essence of these approaches is to deceive yourself by denying (or ignoring) reality. They propose that one should block out challenges, and think of and visualize only positive outcomes to solve everything. This means that when you are feeling sad, anxious, depressed or angry, you should intercept all negative thoughts with positive ones. They advocate repeating affirmations, which are positive statements to help you overcome self-sabotaging and negative thoughts. They claim that by repeating these often, and believing in them, you will start to make positive changes.

There is now much academic and scientific evidence that demonstrates how practising positive thinking in this way can actually be bad for you. Harvard Medical School professor and psychologist Susan David has done a lot of work in this area. In her book, *Emotional Agility: Get Unstuck, Embrace Change and Thrive in Work and Life*, David argues that forcing positive thoughts won't make you happy.

David claims that avoiding negative emotions by either blocking them or trying to avoid them can do more harm than good. She argues that the idea that somehow people should all be happy, and think happy thoughts, and be positive all the time is antithetical to our real happiness. The reality is that life is fragile, and that you are going to get ill, or that you might lose your job or no longer love your job. And there is a lot of research that supports the view that people who strive to be happy actually, over time, become unhappy.

In 2014 Gabriele Oettingen, Professor of Psychology at New York University and the University of Hamburg, published her book, *Rethinking Positive Thinking: Inside the New Science of Motivation*. Oettingen's research showed that in the short term positive thinking is beneficial, but over long periods of time it saps motivation, prevents us from achieving our goals, and leaves us feeling frustrated and stuck.

To really move ahead in life, we need to engage with the world and feel energized – we need to go beyond positive thinking and face the obstacles that stand in our way.

Furthermore, over the last 20 years or so, a new branch of psychology has emerged; 'positive psychology'. It originated out of the University of Pennsylvania with Martin Seligman, who is a professor of psychology. Since it began in 1998, thousands of new research articles and books on the subject have been written, several new academic journals have been published and an international professional association, the International Positive Psychology Association (IPPA), was established.

In essence, positive psychology is the study of what makes life worth living. To push this description further, positive psychology is a scientific approach to studying human thoughts, feelings and behaviour with a focus on strengths as well as weaknesses. It advocates building up the good in life while repairing the bad, and developing the lives of ordinary people to be better, while making those who are struggling more fulfilled.

RETHINKING
'POSITIVE THINKING'

I am not suggesting that the phrase 'positive thinking' should be banished to the annals of history. Rather, we need to rethink what the term really means and reclaim it for the 21ˢᵗ century. With the right definition, understanding and practice, positive thinking can help individuals develop a strong mechanism to cope better with the challenges and maximize on the possibilities that life throws at us all.

The definition I believe to be true and will promote in this book is as follows:

> *Positive thinking is about creating possibilities, and then being better able to assess which ones are realistic and achievable.*

It means being proactive with possibilities that could enrich you. Equally, it means being reactive to those possibilities that might harm you. Thinking positively allows you to assess the risk and the rewards of any possibilities (good or bad) that you are faced with, allowing you to make sensible decisions and develop strategies to cope with them.

When understood from this perspective, positive thinking will help you to make the right decisions and live a more balanced, meaningful and contented life. The positive psychology movement and some of its ideas have been instrumental in helping me to rethink the true meaning of positive thinking that I am promoting here.

Before we start, and for clarity, it is important that I explain the difference between possibility and opportunity, as they have two very distinct meanings, yet they are frequently interchanged in their usage. A 'possibility' implies that something can happen – because you or external circumstances may cause it to happen. An 'opportunity' implies that something is available within boundaries and should be seized. Possibilities – more so than opportunities – can be self-managed because when presented with a possibility it is up to the individual whether to make it happen or not. However, an opportunity depends on circumstances available at the time.

This is the essence of this book and the first step to thinking positively in order to open yourself up to new possibilities. You will be introduced to a wide range of people in these pages. If you have read my other books, you will see that I have had an interesting life so far! CEO of a successful web development company for ten years, suffering a stroke at the age of 41, then becoming a caddie to help my recovery, and now an author of three books and director of one digital agency – a social enterprise and a consultancy practice. Through all these roles, I have met and worked with many CEOs, marketing managers, authors, artists, digital managers, charity bosses and entrepreneurs.

Also, I have come across people I have never met but who have inspired me: an uplifting TED Talk; a memorable

YouTube speech; a successful sportsperson; a Netflix documentary; and so on.

All these individuals have helped me to think outside the box – to think more creatively – which has allowed me to get a different perspective and rethink positive thinking. That then led me to discover the key themes that I will share in this book, to help you unlock new possibilities in your life. That is why the book is split into two parts, *Rethinking positive thinking* and *Opening yourself to new possibilities*.

Through their stories and my own experiences, I am going to explore what these themes are. In each chapter I will share a story, and identify, explore and expand upon a key theme. Part 1 covers the themes of acceptance, purpose, mindset, optimism, strengths, choices, gratitude, negativity, failure and resilience. In Part 2, I focus on values, imagination, dreaming, creativity, goals, identity and emotions. By thinking positively about these core themes and acting on the ideas, insights and thoughts highlighted in each chapter, you will find a different but a very rewarding, type of positive thinking that will help you to open yourself up to new possibilities.

For nine years now I have been using this type of positive thinking, which I am convinced has instigated the presentation of numerous possibilities in both my professional and my personal lives. That is why I came to the conclusion that having a stroke was one of the most positive things that has ever happened to me.

So, let's begin with the person who helped me start the journey that led to the rethinking of positive thinking for the 21st century.

PART 1

RETHINKING POSITIVE THINKING

CHAPTER 1

ACCEPTING YOUR 'NOW'

'Basically, you are f….d'

My neuropsychologist didn't say those exact words, but that's how it felt. Here I was, 18 months on from my stroke, with Dr David Gillespie, as he tried to explain that the damage caused by the stroke meant that I could never be a CEO again.

Yes, I was fully aware that I still had significant issues with speech and memory. However, I was clinging to the idea that one day I would be able to return to the job I loved. And that was what we were talking about, in my counselling session, when he uttered those 'words' (which he did not exactly say!). They stopped me in my tracks.

The session had started well. I told David about the progress I felt I had achieved since our last meeting. Then, as normal, David asked me what was on my mind and what I wanted to talk about. The burning issue, I told him, that had consumed my thoughts recently was just how much I was missing my old life, pre-stroke, as the CEO of a web development company.

In his gentle and calm way, David then explained again (probably for the tenth time over the last 18 months) why returning to my role as CEO was not going to be possible. But this time he explained it slightly differently – and this explanation was the spark that led to this book and so many other positive things in my life.

"Do you want to know what is going on, Neil?" David said. "You are grieving. You are grieving for a part of Neil that died when you had your stroke. Part of your brain was irrevocably damaged – you no longer have the cognitive skills required to run a company. Therefore, you are in a state of grieving for the life you had pre-stroke – the CEO life."

I looked at him and burst into tears!

He was right – I was grieving, and I hated what the stroke had done to me and my family. David then went on to explain that grieving is a process, with a number of stages. He had seen me go through this over the last 18 months. I had spells where I was sad or lonely or anxious or in denial, or angry or confused or frustrated. But then he said this:

"One day, if we continue to work together on it, you hopefully will get to **acceptance**."

And that was the spark. It was a spark that developed into a mindset, which about nine months later allowed me to finally accept my stroke and everything it had left me with.

I accepted that, yes, I had permanent brain damage and I was a stroke survivor but that was OK. And, crucially, I accepted that I would never be a CEO again, and that also was OK.

Once I had accepted what had happened and how I was, new possibilities started to open up in my life.

IT STARTS
HERE

This, in my opinion, is the starting point for positive thinking – acceptance. On paper, accepting the reality of where you are in life sounds like it should be easy. But it is not. As I found out, it took me nearly three years to accept the fact that I would not be a CEO again. During that time, I was either in denial, or trying to convince myself that my damaged brain would miraculously heal itself.

And I think many people could also be in a similar situation, but they don't need to go through a life-threatening event to experience it. For whatever reason, people may be 'stuck' with a view of their life that is stopping them from progressing or finding new possibilities. It might be that they have ideas about setting up a new business or writing a book or moving to another country, and for one reason or another they do nothing, convinced that it is not possible. Or they regret a decision that they have made in the past which has taken them on a path ending up in an unfulfilling job. They believe it is not possible to change that path.

Whatever it is, and whatever you have been through, the starting point to opening yourself up to new possibilities is to *accept* whatever situation you find yourself in.

This is your 'now' – the reality of your life as it currently is.

You might be consumed with anger or regret, so you may be blaming fate, or your poor decisions, or your boss or colleagues, or your loved ones, but whatever it is you just need to stop and accept where you are. When you accept your 'now', you will find a huge weight has been lifted from your shoulders. I realize that this will be incredibly difficult for some people but the only alternative is to keep the status quo and therefore never really move forward in life.

All of this was a result of finally accepting my 'now'. This is the first step: you need to accept what life has thrown at you – good or bad. This is not easy and may not happen straight away. It took me about nine months from that session with David to accept everything about the stroke and its aftermath. For some, it might take longer while for others it might be much quicker. But if you really want to open yourself up to new possibilities, then first you have to accept where you are in life.

Once I totally accepted the stroke and the limitations it had left me with, I was able to allow regret and bitterness to fall away. In fact, the more I accepted it the more I started to see positive things coming from it. This was because I started to 'see' new possibilities – possibilities that I could not see when I was in denial about the reality of my stroke.

TRY TO STOP LOOKING
BACK ON YOUR LIFE
AND INSTEAD LOOK
FORWARD POSITIVELY
AND CREATE A
NEW HISTORY
FOR YOURSELF.

A DIFFERENT
HISTORY

Several years ago I attended an event where the Irish journalist Fergal Keane was talking about his life and his recently published autobiography, *All of These People*. I have always admired him as a journalist – over the years he has reported extensively from many locations around the world including Bosnia, South Africa, Ireland and Rwanda.

That evening, Keane was very open about his personal life. His father was an alcoholic and that eventually killed him. Like his father, he too was an alcoholic. He fought an intense personal battle against alcohol, and struggled with anxiety and depression which all lasted for many years.

During those years he successfully hid his alcoholism from his friends and his employer, the BBC. However, the fear of being found out, perhaps losing his job, and the effects this would have on his family forced him to finally seek help. "I only told the Beeb when the crunch point came," he recalls. "I came back from a trip to Spain and I called my direct boss and explained that I was in real trouble, and needed some time off."

That call led him to meeting someone who showed him a way out of drinking. He stopped drinking in June 1999 and has not had a drink since. In the early days of his sobriety he was told by a counsellor that he had a chance to stop the cycle of alcoholism that had plagued his family. He did not need to die like his father had, from alcoholism. Crucially, the counsellor told him that he did not need to pass on his unhappiness to his son. And then the counsellor said this to him:

> *The history can stop here and now. It can become a different history.*

That statement is positive thinking in action. Accept and acknowledge the difficulties and challenges that you have faced so far in your life. Then try to stop looking back on your life and instead look forward positively and create a new history for yourself.

The first step after having accepted your 'now' is to discover your purpose. And to help you do so, I want to introduce you to Kari in the next chapter.

DISCOVERING MEANING

To explore the effects of 'purpose' on positive thinking I want to share the story of a remarkable young woman called Kari Spence. Now 27 years old, Kari embodies probably one of the most important aspects of thinking positively.

In 2009, aged 18, Kari got the opportunity to travel to Rwanda with a group of 15 other young people from a local youth club. The aim of the trip was to help build a playground for a school in Kigali, Rwanda's capital city. For Kari, this was a life-changing experience. She completely fell in love with the country and the people, and she knew with certainty she wanted to return to Rwanda.

Then, in 2010, Kari deferred her entry to study physical education teaching at university in the UK and headed back to Rwanda. For three months she lived in a rural village with a local family and lived the life of a local Rwandan. She ate traditional Rwandan food, and lived with limited water in a house that had no electricity. She volunteered at the local school, where she taught English and introduced different sports to primary pupils.

During this trip Kari was taken to another small rural village, Gako, around an hour's drive from the capital, to visit Faith and Hope Primary School. When she arrived at the school she was shocked at how many pupils were squeezed into one classroom, how few school supplies they had, and how dirty and malnourished the pupils were. She immediately knew this was where she could make a huge difference.

After that, Kari made two trips a year to the school, working closely with the teachers, particularly developing their physical education and health and wellbeing programmes. Six years on from her first trip to Rwanda, Kari founded the charity 'Together in Sport Rwanda' (TiSR). Over the years TiSR has set up and run a variety of different projects directly helping improve the lives of 500 children in the Faith and Hope community.

The projects are many and varied. For example, there is the 'Friends of Faith and Hope' programme, where donors contribute monthly to a general fund for buying school supplies, paying toward the entire school's health insurance and a crisis fund that helps families identified as having the most hardship.

Additionally, in 2015 Kari put out an appeal on social media to raise money to build the first kitchen for the school

– it was a huge success. 'The Food Programme', which aims to provide every child attending school with one hot meal per day, was introduced in the spring of 2016, following the completion of the kitchen.

I helped Kari when she was starting the TiSR project and had a catch-up meeting with her before December 2018. As ever, she was positive about TiSR and the work the charity was doing. And, she informed me that she was moving to Rwanda to be a teacher and work on the TiSR project permanently in January 2019.

She explained, "I love the country and its people, because of their enthusiasm and attitude toward life. Even with the very little the children have they are the happiest and most resilient children I have been lucky to work alongside. When I first went to Rwanda it changed my outlook on life; the work I do for the charity, it doesn't feel like work because I get so much enjoyment, positivity and inspiration from the people I'm working with. Rwanda and this charity have given my life purpose and meaning, and I'm excited about what the future holds."

The word '**purpose**' summarizes perfectly why Kari embodies such an important aspect of positive thinking.

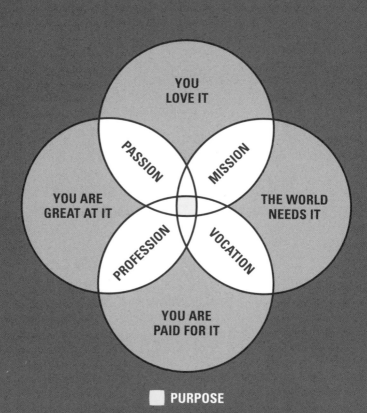

WHY IS PURPOSE
SO IMPORTANT?

Identifying 'purpose' provides you with a stable foundation and a sense of direction, both of which are integral to a positive outlook on life. A solid foundation allows you to be more resilient and bounce back from adversity. A sense of direction allows you to set goals.

For some, purpose is connected to their occupation – meaningful, satisfying work. For others, their purpose is connected to responsibilities to their family or friends. Others seek purpose through spirituality or religious beliefs. Some people may find their purpose clearly expressed in all these aspects of life. Wherever it is and where you find it, purpose can guide life decisions, influence behaviour, shape goals, offer a sense of direction and create meaning.

Purpose will be unique for everyone; what you identify as your path will be different from other people's. What's more, your purpose can actually shift and change throughout life in response to the evolving priorities and fluctuations of your own experiences.

One of the best descriptions of purpose came from Dan Buettner, a *National Geographic* Fellow and *New York Times* bestselling author. In 2009, Buettner gave a TED Talk titled, "How to Live to Be 100+". He talked about his research on the world's Blue Zones. These are areas where people live inordinately long, healthy lives. The Blue Zone with the longest disability-free life expectancy in the world is the Japanese island of Okinawa and its surrounding islands. In this region, people routinely live beyond 100 years of age. And at this age, they are still physically capable, fully alert and involved in the community around them. They work in their gardens and play with their great-grandchildren, and when they die it generally happens quickly and in their sleep. Their rates of disease are many times lower than those in much of the rest of the world.

Interestingly, Okinawans don't have a word for retirement. What they have is *ikigai*, which roughly translated means 'passion' or 'reason for living'. When he conducted his study with the Okinawans, one of the questions in Buettner's questionnaire was, "What is your *ikigai*?" Nearly all of the people were able to answer immediately. For a 102-year-old karate master, his *ikigai* was to teach his martial art. For a 100-year-old fisherman, it was bringing fish back to his family three days a week. For a 102-year-old woman, it was to spend time with her great-great-granddaughter. These were their 'reasons for living' – their *ikigai*; their purpose.

Thinking positively will help you find your *ikigai* – your purpose.

Identifying your purpose is crucial for thinking positively. A good starting point for this is the answers to these four simple but thought-provoking questions:

1. **What do you love?**
   The answer to this is your passion.

2. **What are you good at?**
   The answer to this is your mission.

3. **What can you be paid for?**
   The answer to this is your profession.

4. **What does the world need?**
   The answer to this is your talent.

If you can answer those four questions, then you have probably identified your current purpose, your *ikigai*.

GET INTO YOUR
TIME MACHINE

If you are currently struggling to find direction and your purpose in life, then imagine jumping into a time machine and arriving at the year you turn 75. Then, ask yourself these five questions:

How, and for what, do I want to be remembered?

By whom do I want to be remembered?

Which achievements and personal strengths do I want others to talk about?

When I look back on the life I have lived, am I satisfied with it?

Am I living the life today that will mean that I achieve this when I am 75?

The answer to these questions should help you to identify whether you are living according to your values, whether you are achieving your goals and whether your life is going in the direction you want it to. Importantly, if you answered 'no' to questions 4 and 5, then think about the changes you can make to ensure that you are heading in the right direction. This direction will help you achieve your goals, so that you can look back on a life well lived when you are 75. Make sure these changes are realistic and within your control.

Now, this is the crucial bit. Write down your answers and look at them in six months or a year to see if you have made progress toward achieving your goals. If you feel you are drifting off track, then remember the 75-year-old version of you and revise your goals as you learn more about yourself and the person you really want to be. All of this will not happen overnight, but it is a gradual realization that takes place over time.

Many people find that thinking about their life's purpose seems too abstract or uncomfortable. If you are not a spiritual person and don't believe in some higher order of things, thinking about the purpose of your life can seem airy-fairy. For others, it can be very difficult and painful to face the way you have lived your life so far. If you are in either or both of these situations, don't worry – many other people are in the same boat.

But don't underestimate the benefit of believing that you are making a difference in some way, and that your life has purpose. This is an important part of thinking positively and it is fundamental to your wellbeing. Kari Spence's story is testament to this because once she found a purpose, her life became enriched and, at the same time, the lives of the children she works with in Rwanda were enriched. For me, Kari's story also demonstrates the power of positive thinking.

CHAPTER 3

DEVELOPING A GROWTH MINDSET

MINDSET

It is widely accepted that Bill Gates is one of the most successful entrepreneurs the world has ever seen. He co-founded Microsoft, with Paul Allen, in 1975 and helped it grow to become the most valuable company in the world (at least, until early 2019). Starting with only two employees, Microsoft has grown to more than 134,000 employees today with offices all around the world. Its technology is used daily by millions of people and it has shaped how we all work and spend our personal time.

One of Gates's greatest strengths has been his ability to predict what the world of work and leisure will look like in the future. In 1999, Gates wrote a book, *Business @ the Speed of Thought*, in which he made 15 bold predictions that, at the time, sounded far-fetched.

For example, he predicted that: "People will carry around small devices that allow them to constantly stay in touch and do electronic business from wherever they are. They will be able to check the news, see flights they have booked, get information from financial markets, and do just about anything else on these devices."

And what do we see around us today – smartphones, smartwatches, smart speakers like the Amazon Echo, and Apple's virtual assistant Siri all of which give users a way to have all of their information on hand at all times.

He also predicted this: "Devices will have smart advertising. They will know your purchasing trends and will display advertisements that are tailored toward your preferences."

And what happens today when you use Facebook or search Google – there are tailored adverts and content aimed right at the things you are interested in.

However, Gates did make some predictions that were, putting it mildly, wrong!

"I see little commercial potential for the internet for the next 10 years", Gates allegedly said at one Comdex trade event in 1994.

Indeed, in his 1995 book, *The Road Ahead*, Gates wrote that the internet was a novelty that would eventually give way to something much better: "Today's Internet is not the information highway I imagine, although you can think of it as the beginning of the highway."

However, in the months between finishing the book, publishing it and getting it into bookstores, Gates realized that the internet was taking off after all. He issued Microsoft's famous "The Internet tidal wave" memo and reoriented the company in that direction, situating the internet as a fundamental part of Microsoft going forward.

All of this shows one of the main attributes that has made him so successful – he has a 'growth', rather than a 'fixed', mindset. He is fascinated by new things and he loves to learn, and that is why so many of his predictions turned out to be correct. However, Gates also demonstrates that when he got a prediction wrong, he accepted it, changed his view and turned it into a positive thing.

In his book, *Business @the Speed of Thought: Succeeding in the Digital Economy*, he said: "Once you embrace unpleasant news not as a negative but as evidence of a need for change, you aren't defeated by it."

By embracing unpleasant news, Gates was demonstrating a **growth mindset**, which is a fundamental part of positive thinking. His mindset has significantly contributed to him being such a successful entrepreneur and businessman.

"ONCE YOU EMBRACE UNPLEASANT NEWS NOT AS A NEGATIVE BUT AS EVIDENCE OF A NEED FOR CHANGE, YOU AREN'T DEFEATED BY IT."

Bill Gates
*Business @ the Speed of Thought:
Succeeding in the Digital Economy*

FIXED AND
GROWTH MINDSETS

If you look into fixed and growth mindsets you will find that Carol Dweck, Professor of Psychology at Stanford University, is well known in this area. She is one of the leading psychologists in this field. In 2007, Dweck published *Mindset: The New Psychology of Success*, and to date her book has sold well over two million copies worldwide. In it, she explains the differences between people who have a fixed mindset versus those with a growth mindset. According to Dweck, mindset determines the way we deal with tough situations and setbacks. It also determines our willingness to improve ourselves and how we think about our personality, what we are passionate about and our goals.

A predominately fixed mindset means that you believe your attributes, intelligence and abilities are inherently fixed and unchangeable. In other words, you're as smart as you'll ever be. This leads to the desire to look smart in front of other people and a tendency to avoid challenges, to be defensive and to give up easily. A person with a fixed mindset will ignore useful negative feedback and feel threatened by the success of others. The outcome of all of this is that you achieve less than your full potential.

However, if you have a predominately growth mindset, then you see things differently. You see your level, of intelligence, skill, talent and success as the starting point, with the capacity to grow. You believe that there are numerous stepping stones toward development and improvement. This mindset is founded on the belief that your initial qualities can be cultivated and grown with dedication, time and hard work. You believe you can get better and smarter, and you can be flexible.

This leads to a desire to learn, embrace challenges, persist in the face of setbacks, learn from criticism and find lessons or inspiration in the success of others. This will lead you to study, to learn and to put the work into expanding your mind in order to become more intelligent.

Going back to Gates, in 2015 he posted an article on his blog, *Gates Notes*. He explained that Dweck's book had a big impact on him. In the last paragraph of his article, he says this: "The greatest virtue of the book is that you can't help but ask yourself things like, 'Which areas have I always looked at through a fixed-mindset lens?'"

If you want to use positive thinking to help you grow and develop, then you need to examine those areas of your life where you have had a predominately fixed mindset. To do this, you need to be aware of the mindset you adopt in a given situation because this will affect your behaviour and can greatly influence the outcome of a situation or any challenges you face.

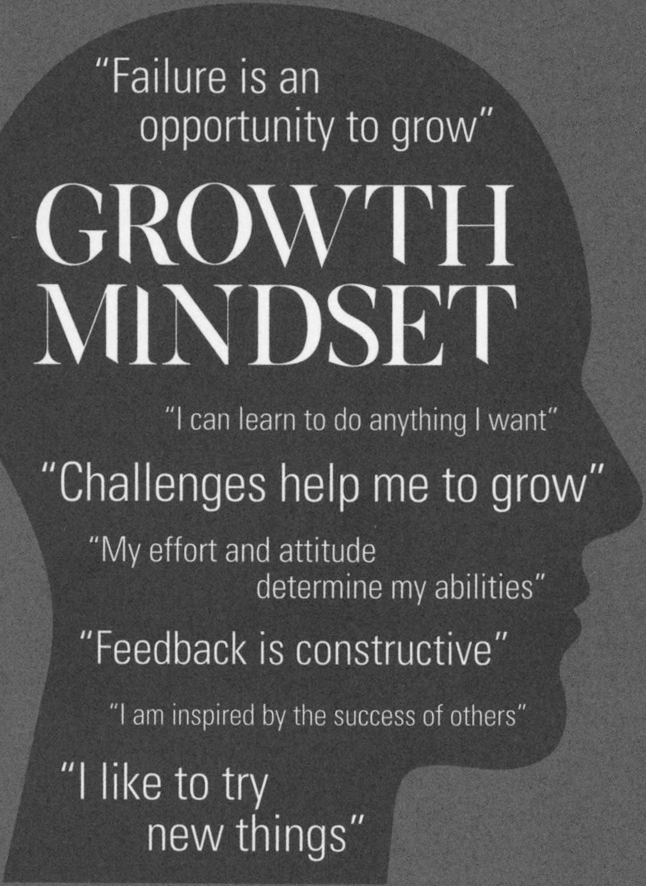
"Failure is an opportunity to grow"
GROWTH MINDSET
"I can learn to do anything I want"
"Challenges help me to grow"
"My effort and attitude determine my abilities"
"Feedback is constructive"
"I am inspired by the success of others"
"I like to try new things"

"Failure is the limit of my abilities"

FIXED MINDSET

"I'm either good at it or I'm not"

"My abilities are unchanging"

"I can either do it, or I can't"

"I don't like to be challenged"

"My potential is predetermined"

"When I'm frustrated, I give up"

"Feedback and criticism are personal"

"I stick to what I know"

MINDSET AND
BEHAVIOUR

There are four main ways that your mindset affects your behaviour.

The goals you decide to pursue

If you have a fixed mindset then you are likely to focus on performance goals. Your ability can be measured easily in that you either meet your goals or you don't. For a sportsperson this might be running a 10k in a certain time. For a sales rep, it could be selling a number of products in any given month. Meeting set criteria means that your skill or ability is validated. Unfortunately, the reverse is also true. If you fall short on that criterion, you feel you are not skilful and lack ability. Basically, you are exercising a kind of 'black or white' thinking – you are skilful, talented and clever, or you are not.

However, if you have a growth mindset then you will be more interested in setting learning goals, which means you focus on gaining competence in an area first, and then mastering it. It is more about growing and learning than passing and failing or winning and losing.

How you respond to failure

When you fail with a fixed mindset you may feel helpless and hopeless. If the performance goal is low, then you can become anxious, lose self-confidence and run out of steam. You may even feel that nothing will ever change. Ironically, when you achieve goals, you can still become stressed and anxious because once you have achieved your goal you feel the need to keep performing at this level to maintain the belief that you are clever, skilful and talented.

For someone with a growth mindset, failure is not a big thing. You focus on learning from the experience, which will help you to do better next time. You are far more willing to listen to advice and try new solutions in order to improve. You believe that doing badly in a physical or mental challenge is not because you lack dedication or that you are stupid – you just accept that today was not your day.

Making an effort

If you have a fixed mindset and have put in a huge amount of effort, then you feel you are less capable than you had thought. You subscribe to the statement: 'If I have to work hard it must mean that I'm not clever.'

The opposite applies to those with a growth mindset, who correlate effort to success. The harder you work and the more effort you put in, the more likely you are to succeed. You tend to be persistent and refuse to give up when faced with disappointment. You accept that success rarely happens overnight and will require determination and effort.

Fixed or flexible solutions

When faced with a problem, fixed-mindset people typically keep doing the same thing and repeating the same behaviour. Finally, they give up instead of seeking alternative solutions to the problem.

People with a growth mindset aren't so easily defeated. They think of problems and challenges as opportunities to try something new and are willing to look for different solutions. By doing this, they are far more likely to be successful in the end.

HOW TO DEVELOP
A GROWTH MINDSET

Looking back to the time after I had my stroke, I realize that in the two to three years immediately afterward I was demonstrating a fixed mindset in everything I was trying to do. So, for example, my speech therapist would set weekly tasks to help with the recovery of my speech. However, if I could not do the task immediately, rather than persevering, I would give up. I would then feel hopeless, stressed and anxious.

But with time and a lot of help, I started to focus on areas in my life where I could see achievable goals – goals that I thought were realistic. I was motivated to try to achieve them. However, I accepted that in order to achieve these goals I would have to work hard and put in a lot of effort. A good example is the first book I wrote, *Changing Course*. Once I had the idea for the book, I was very motivated to write it. I accepted that I might not be able to complete it and get it published but I realized that was not the point. I was more focused on how far I could get with it. I was using a growth mindset.

Here are tips and suggestions to help you develop a growth mindset. Yes, some may be easier than others, but try them, persevere, practise and don't give up!

- **Accept your imperfections**
  Work on improving and developing those skills you don't find so easy. Don't simply give up just because you're not the best at something.

- **Focus on your growth rather than speed**
  Take time to explore ideas and develop new skills that help you improve, allowing for complications or setbacks along the way. You won't gain anything by rushing through tasks half-heartedly.

- **Think of challenges or failure as part of the learning process**
  Everyone faces obstacles, challenges and defeats, but the way that you respond to them can make the difference between success and failure. Try to take on these challenges and use them as an opportunity for growth.

- **Value the process over the end goal**
  Enjoy the entire process and don't just focus on the outcome.

- **Always set new goals**
  As soon as you've achieved one goal, set another. Always set out to learn more and never be complacent. You'll have a sense of purpose knowing you are constantly working toward something better.

If you think positively and start to action some of the suggestions in this chapter, you are already demonstrating more of a growth mindset. This should make you confident in your ability to adapt, to improve and to face the challenges you encounter in a constructive way.

When you are using a growth mindset, you will find yourself more optimistic in your thinking. As you will see in the next chapter, being optimistic will be the springboard for thinking and acting positively.

THE
IMPORTANCE
OF OPTIMISM

On 26 November 2018, I watched on live TV the successful landing of NASA's InSight probe on Mars. The mission's purpose is to help scientists explore and learn about the core, crust and mantle of Mars. This information will enable NASA scientists to identify how Mars was formed at the dawn of the solar system 4.6 billion years ago.

The InSight spacecraft was launched on a rocket from California on 5 May 2018. Moving away from Earth at a speed of 6,200 miles per hour, InSight covered a distance of 33.9 million miles to reach Mars in less than seven months. When it arrived in Mars's orbit, the spacecraft hurtled into the thin Martian atmosphere at 12,300 miles per hour, and then slowed down to just about five miles per hour before it hit the surface. It deployed a parachute and fired 12 retro-thrusters to cushion its landing. It used a heat shield for protection as the surrounding air slammed into the spacecraft, heating it up to 2,700°F. NASA calls the entry, descent and landing phase of its Mars missions the 'seven minutes of terror'.

Over the years, thousands of scientists and engineers worked on this mission. This has involved: prelaunch activities including designing and building InSight; the launch involving the rocket that contained InSight; planning the flight path; the approach and the final trajectory; the landing; and the surface operations when InSight had landed.

Landing a probe on Mars remains a very tricky business for scientists and engineers: only 40% of missions so far have been successful. Some scientists and engineers have worked on this mission for decades, with no guarantee that it would succeed. It was also incredibly expensive, and if it failed it would be a significant setback for NASA. The risk that something could go wrong, at any stage of the mission, was extremely high. For example, the flight path had to be adjusted several times to make sure that InSight was flying at the right speed and in the direction. If one scientist's flight-path calculations had been wrong, chances are that the probe would have missed Mars's orbit.

It is safe to say that people who work on the InSight mission need a very special skill set. They need to be confident in their ability, resilient and actioned-oriented in the face of adversity, and very flexible in their thinking.

But, perhaps the most important quality is **optimism**. As Anne Kinney, then Director of the Solar System Exploration Division at NASA's Goddard Space Flight Center, said, "If you have a method or idea and you believe it works, you have to be optimistic about it. Optimism is the number-one thing."

And when you think about it, that makes so much sense. Working on any NASA mission, where there will be so many challenges, failures, disappointments and frustrations, requires staff to be optimistic. Being optimistic means that these individuals think in a more positive and flexible way. This leads them to believe that problems and challenges are solvable so that they are prepared to commit to weeks or even years working on them.

And that is why Kinney said optimism is "the number-one thing" required at NASA because staff have to believe that it is their responsibility to make a mission successful, and not the responsibility of others or external factors.

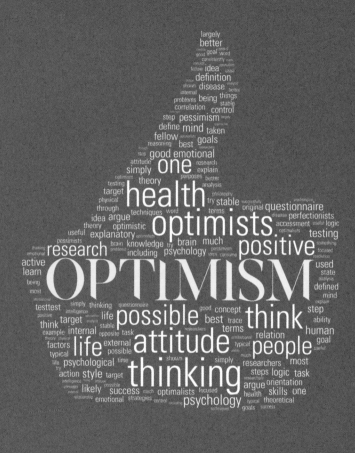

GLASS HALF-FULL
OR HALF-EMPTY

I am sure that most people, at some point, have been asked whether they see their life as the proverbial glass that is either half-empty or half-full. The answer to this question will tell you a lot about your own personality. If you see the glass as half-empty, you're generally considered a pessimist. Viewing the glass as half-full, then, makes you an optimist.

Pessimists have a generalized sense of doubt and hesitancy, characterized by the anticipation of negative outcomes. They expect the worst and overestimate the risks, assuming that things will go wrong.

On the other hand, optimists approach problems from a position of empowerment. Some see overcoming adversity as a challenge, one that they will gladly attempt to conquer. Optimistic people view failure as being temporary and attribute it to the situation or as a matter of circumstance.

There is now growing evidence showing the benefits, both physical and psychological, of being an optimist rather than a pessimist.

- Optimists experience less distress than pessimists when dealing with difficulties in their lives. For example, they suffer much less anxiety and depression.

- Optimists tend to deal with problems, rather than just avoiding them, by using acceptance, humour and positive reframing (putting the situation in the best possible light).

- Optimists don't tend to use denial. By not sticking their heads in the sand they face up to difficult situations and challenges, while pessimists often attempt to distance themselves from the problem.

- Optimists don't give up easily even when faced with serious adversity, whereas pessimists are more likely to anticipate disaster and give up as a result.

- Optimists have a higher level of life satisfaction and increased wellbeing. They are more likely to look after themselves physically and mentally.

It is crucial that an optimist has a sense of realism. Therefore, while their attitude leads them to take risks, they need to act in a way that increases the chance of a positive outcome.

THINKING POSITIVELY
ABOUT PESSIMISM

For many years it was thought that optimism or pessimism was hardwired into behaviour and that people had to deal with how they were because there was no way to change it. However, contemporary science says otherwise. The person leading research into what he calls 'learned optimism' is Dr Martin Seligman, Professor of Psychology, University of Pennsylvania.

Seligman argues that anyone can make use of learned optimism, regardless of how pessimistic their outlook. To do this Seligman developed a test in conjunction with Stanford University to identify an individual's base level of optimism. The test contains 48 questions and is used to determine an individual's base level of optimism.

The next step is to assess reactions to negative situations. Seligman's approach is the 'ABCDE' model of learned optimism, which stands for Adversity, Belief, Consequence, Disputation and Energization. Using Seligman's model could help you to be more optimistic in many situations:

Adversity
Think about a recent problem or difficult challenge you have faced.

Belief

Make a note of your thoughts and feelings when thinking about the problem. It is very important to be as honest as you can and not 'edit' your feelings.

Consequence

Thoughtfully consider the consequences and behaviours that emerged from the thoughts you have noted. Analyse whether these thoughts resulted in positive actions that helped you overcome the problem, or whether they kept you from doing that.

Disputation

Dispute and challenge your beliefs. Think about the thoughts you noted and look for examples from your life that prove those beliefs wrong.

Energization

Consider how you feel now that you have challenged and disputed your beliefs. Do you feel more energized and motivated? Do you feel that the problem you originally thought was unsolvable is actually solvable? Has it made you more optimistic about challenging your beliefs and changed your thoughts about the original problem?

By using Seligman's approach, people who are more optimistic at the outset can further improve their emotional health, and those who are initially more pessimistic can benefit by lowering their chances of experiencing symptoms of stress, anxiety and depression. Evidence from Seligman's research, and from other psychologists who have studied optimism and pessimism, demonstrates that this simple but very effective technique can encourage optimism. Still, although it might sound easy on paper, that doesn't mean you're going to learn how to be an optimist overnight.

However, some psychologists argue that learned optimism training programmes, like Seligman's, are less about teaching people to become more optimistic and more about reducing pessimism. In addition, psychologists have suggested that optimism could have a negative side as it might encourage people to take health risks and engage in risky activities because they underestimate their own level of danger. And there is some merit in those claims.

Saying all of that, though, most studies support the idea that there is a positive connection between optimism and overall good health. However, learning and practising optimism is about more than just improving your wellbeing or helping you to cope with stress, low self-esteem or anxiety. Seligman suggests it can help you find your purpose and is invaluable for discovering a meaningful life. And that is why optimism plays an important part in positive thinking. If you have a pessimistic outlook on life, then optimism can be learned and put into practice.

Going back to the NASA scientists and engineers, maybe the reason these people commit so much of their lives to trying to solve extremely complex scientific and engineering challenges is that it provides them with a feeling that their lives are meaningful. Their enduring optimism helps them to remain optimistic in the face of all challenges, and that is a core element of positive thinking.

CHAPTER 5

THE POWER
OF STRENGTHS

STRENGTHS

I would like to introduce you to one of the most prolific inventors of our time, a name you've probably never heard: Yoshiro Nakamatsu or, as he likes to be called, Dr NakaMats. He is the holder of over 3,500 patents for his inventions.

The 3,500 patents he has include the CD, the DVD, the fax machine, the taxi meter, the digital watch, the karaoke machine, CinemaScope, spring-loaded shoes, fuel-cell-powered boots, an invisible 'B-bust bra', a water powered engine, the world's tiniest air conditioner, a self-defence wig that can be swung at an attacker, a pillow that prevents drivers from nodding off behind the wheel, an automated version of the popular Japanese game pachinko, a musical golf putter that pings when the ball is struck properly, and a perpetual motion machine that runs on heat and cosmic energy, to name just a few!

In an interview, Dr NakaMats described his 'creativity process', which includes listening to music and diving – where he comes up with his best ideas and even records them while underwater. Nakamatsu claims that he benefits from a lack of oxygen to the brain during his dives, making inventions "0.5 seconds before death". He also claims that his Calm Room, a bathroom constructed without nails and tiled in 24-carat gold, encourages creative thinking by blocking television and radio waves.

But what has Dr NakaMats got to do with positive thinking? Well, he is exceptionally creative and has dedicated his life to putting that creativity into action as an inventor. Creativity is his key strength, to the extent that he has developed his own creativity process to help him come up with more inventions. So, using your strengths more frequently, like Dr NakaMats, you will think and act more positively.

WHEN YOU USE
YOUR STRENGTHS,
IT JUST FEELS
RIGHT.

A BIT ABOUT
STRENGTHS

A strength is a personal attribute that energizes you and enables you to perform at your best. A strength is also a strong attribute or an inherent asset. Using strengths enables people to consistently provide a seamless performance in a specific activity. Your strengths are innate and unique to you, and leveraging them can improve performance. When you use your strengths, it just feels right.

Over the last 20 years there has been a boom in strength-based tools to help identify dominant strengths. Probably the two most popular tools are the Gallup StrengthsFinder (now CliftonStrengths) and VIA (Values in Action) Character Strengths.

Through interviewing 1.7 million individuals from various fields and roles – executives, salespeople, teachers, doctors, lawyers, students, administrators, manual labourers and nurses, to name but a few – Gallup was able to identify 34 key strengths or 'talents themes'. From this they developed an assessment tool, the StrengthsFinder, which allows anyone to identify their dominant thinking patterns, which Gallup calls Strength Themes. To date, over 20 million people around the world have tried these tools.

Let me give you some examples of a talent:

> **A talent for empathy.** You walk into a room where a meeting is in progress and, very quickly, you pick up on the atmosphere. If the meeting is going badly, you *feel* the tension in the air. The key is that you sense the tension without anyone actually saying anything.
>
> **A talent for action.** There's one person who's desperate for everyone to reach a decision. They have a talent for getting things done quickly.
>
> **A talent for focus.** Meanwhile, there's also a person who is getting stressed that the agenda is changing, and that the meeting is now covering lots of new subjects. That person has a talent for concentrating on one thing at a time.

Talents are also referred to as character strengths, for example in the VIA classification of 24 character strengths. These 24 character strengths fall under the six broad categories of wisdom, courage, humanity, justice, temperance and transcendence. Typically, each of us has a unique set of signature strengths that we frequently use.

Whether you see your strengths as innate talents or character strengths, when exercised, your strengths tend to energize and excite you – bringing you more fully alive and helping you to meet the demands of your daily life.

Using your strengths in the right way can bring you into a state of 'flow' when doing any activity. When you experience flow, you lose track of time. You don't feel self-conscious and you feel that what you're doing is intrinsically rewarding and enjoyable because you are using your strengths to maximum impact.

Not only does playing to your strengths improve your wellbeing, it can help you improve your performance at work, making you more engaged and more likely to achieve your goals. These are very compelling reasons to identify your strengths and start using them more, both at home and in the workplace. Using your strengths often is beneficial for you in a number of ways.

- **Increased resilience**
  Using your strengths frequently will help you to bounce back better from adversity.

- **Increased confidence**
  Using your strengths more is associated with increased self-esteem and self-efficacy.

- **Less stress**
  By using your strengths, over time you will suffer less stress.

- **Increased vitality**
  Using your strengths is associated with high levels of positive energy.

- **Goal achievement**
  People who use their strengths are more likely to attain their goals.

- **Increased happiness**
  Using your strengths can make you happier and contribute to your wellbeing.

So, the obvious question is, how do you identify your strengths?

IDENTIFYING
YOUR STRENGTHS

There's a huge range of tools, books and online assessments and methods to help you identify your strengths. With regard to online tools, the two I found really helpful were VIA Character Strengths and the Gallup StrengthsFinder. The books I would recommend are *The Strengths Book* by Sally Bibbs and *StrengthsFinder 2.0* by Tom Rath and Gallup. The latter gives you information about the StrengthsFinder tool and its history, and describes in detail the 34 individual strengths. Both are brilliant books.

In addition, to help you get the most out of these tools and books, I would recommend that you have at least one discussion with a mentor or coach who understands these tools. These coaches can help you better understand what your strengths are and how to maximize the impact they can have in your life.

If this all feels a bit formal, or if you don't like doing this kind of assessment, a simple way of uncovering your strengths is to ask your friends and family – those who are closest to you – what *they* think your strengths are.

By this, I mean the things they've observed that you are naturally good at. Don't ask them about your knowledge and skills, but about your innate strengths. Some examples could be:

- you are really adaptable and can spin many plates at once
- you are fantastic at communicating, whether one-on-one or in front of a big crowd
- you are driven to get things done
- you have a wonderful ability to get the most out of people
- you dislike conflict and try to bring people together
- you love creativity and invention
- you have a passion for learning and exploring new things

And if you really think about it, you'll probably find that you already know exactly what you're naturally good at. So, along with considering what your family and friends tell you, sit down and ask yourself which aspects of your current job, role or hobby fill you with excitement. In which areas do you get the most positive feedback from others, and which tasks do you feel really comfortable doing? These are probably the areas in which you are using your strengths.

MY STROKE
AND STRENGTHS

After I had my stroke, I had significant cognitive impairment in a number of areas. However, it became apparent fairly quickly that my natural strengths had remained largely intact. I was still bursting with ideas and keen to put them into practice; I could still pick up the mood of a room very quickly; and I could still see how to achieve potential outcomes by connecting up ideas and people.

My limitations, however, were far more pronounced than they had been before the stroke. Organizing and planning my week was very challenging; focusing on one thing, even for a short time, was very difficult; and scenario planning was virtually impossible.

The first time I did the StrengthsFinder assessment was three years before I had my stroke. So, to see if I'd retained my strengths or if they had changed, I repeated the assessment a few years after my stroke. And do you know what, the results were the same! My strengths were the same as they'd been before the stroke.

This emphasized that I should focus more than ever on developing and using my strengths. By doing so, I was able to achieve far more than if I worked on my limitations. I still do this today. And the results are still the same: whenever I am using my strengths, I feel more resilient and confident and achieve my goals more easily. Everything feels more natural and enjoyable. Crucially, this leads to me thinking positively about the goals I have set myself and the challenges I am facing.

Identifying your own strengths and then using them so that you also can set realistic and achievable goals and overcome challenges in your own life helps you become dramatically more positive in your thinking.

CHAPTER 6

MAKING CHOICES

CHOICES

On 1 August 1996, at the Atlanta Olympic Games, Michael Johnson set a new world record for the 200-metre sprint of 19.32 seconds. In 1997 Johnson began appearing in Nike television advertisements in which he was billed as the 'World's fastest man' as a result of his 200 metres world record. Johnson's record time was not beaten for another 12 years, until the Beijing Olympics in 2008, when Usain Bolt ran the distance in 19.28 seconds, setting a new world record.

Fast forward to 2018 when, aged 50, Johnson had a stroke. Initially he could not walk or move his left leg. The doctors told him that the best chance of recovery was to get into physical therapy immediately. So, two days after the stroke he got out of bed and with the help of a physiotherapist he slowly walked around the ward – ironically the distance he covered that day was around 200 metres and it took him around 15 minutes.

Three months later, in an interview, he talked about the irony of taking 15 minutes to complete a distance that had taken him only 19.32 seconds 22 years earlier. He said: "Ordinarily that would be very disconcerting and I would have no hope – having been the fastest person in the world at that distance – but I was very encouraged. With every step I took, I could feel myself relearning. For the next few weeks I went back into an Olympic mindset and focused on having the best training session I could each day, and using it to be better and get better."

This is such an inspirational story and I am certain that many people will admire Johnson's attitude and determination, which eventually helped him to make a full recovery. However, there was one thing that stood out for me. At the point when he was told that he'd suffered a stroke, and during the next few days, Johnson knew he had to make a **choice**.

He could feel sorry for himself and become consumed by uncertainty. Or, he could accept that he'd had a stroke and *choose* to focus on his recovery, not on the uncertainty of what the future might hold. Using his 'Olympian mindset' (Johnson's words) he thought positively about how he would make the best recovery, even though he did not know what the end of his recovery would look like.

But he did not procrastinate, nor did he ignore what the doctors were saying about the seriousness of what had happened. Crucially, by thinking positively, he took the facts, listened to the experts and made a choice to walk as soon as he could, however disheartening or scary that was.

IT'S ALL
OVER HERE

Positive thinking is about making daily choices and acting on them, even though you may often have no idea what the outcome might be. You look at the facts as you see them, take advice if required and make choices based on that. That is positive thinking. Some of these choices will be very difficult; other times they will be easier or more obvious. But what is crucial is that you don't procrastinate or ignore the difficult choices – thinking positively about difficult and challenging choices will help you get through these times.

The book by Cyndi Crother, *Catch! A Fishmonger's Guide to Greatness*, is based on the experiences of the staff of a very famous fish market in Seattle called Pike Place Fish Market. The fish market is a dynamic and exciting environment to visit, but what has made it stand out is the set of beliefs that the fishmongers live by. Put simply, they are driven by a desire to make a positive difference to their own lives and to the lives of visitors, colleagues and competitors. This philosophy influences the way they act and behave.

At Pike Place Fish Market, the mantra is 'It's all over here', and to staff this means: 'I am responsible for what I experience and how I react to whatever occurs in my life.' This powerful little statement is all about making choices in life. It is very powerful and positive to realize and accept that everything you think and do is your choice. Nobody else's. Not only does that mean that you cope better at difficult times, but also that you are acting in a positive way by making choices. As long as you accept this and are willing to commit to making choices – however difficult and painful they might be – then you are using positive thinking in the right, helpful and beneficial way.

"THE PARADOX OF CHOICE."

Barry Schwartz
Psychologist and Professor of Social Theory
and Social Action at Swarthmore College

TOO MUCH
CHOICE

However, there is a big caveat attached to what I have just said. There is growing and compelling evidence that having too much choice can have negative effects. Barry Schwartz, a psychologist and Professor of Social Theory and Social Action at Swarthmore College and an acknowledged world expert on the psychology of choice, gave a fascinating TED Talk, "The paradox of choice". In it, he explained that some choice is good but that doesn't necessarily mean that more choice is better. Schwartz calls this "the tyranny of choice".

Over the last 20 or 30 years we have come to be bombarded with choice. Walk into your local supermarket and look at how much choice you have – numerous brands of coffee, a ridiculous number of varieties of breakfast cereal, and half an aisle selling only bread! Switch on the TV and see just how many channels there are for you to choose from. Choice is now a given in our lives and most of us take it for granted because choice means we have freedom. It helps us express who we are as an individual.

However, as Schwartz highlighted, too much choice can cause us problems. In order to make a choice, you have to process a lot of information to try to make the best choice. A good example was when I recently started the process of buying a new car. On paper this sounds like an enjoyable process, but it turned out to be anything but. I was staggered by the choice of so many cars that were on offer. And so I spent many a weekend traipsing from showroom to showroom. Finally, I decided on the car I thought would meet my needs. And then I met the sales person! I must have spent at least a couple of hours with him considering options like performance, diesel or petrol, manual or automatic, the colour, the interior fabric and the wheels I wanted. Then, he proceeded to explain all the finance options that were available to me and the insurance coverage I could choose. It was an exhausting process, and when I finally left the showroom, rather than feeling happy, my mind started questioning whether I had chosen the right wheels, should I have gotten a sunroof, and maybe I should put down a bigger deposit! I was stressed and tired.

You see, although the majority of the options were not that important, I still needed to make a choice. And this is the important bit. As the volume and the complexity of the information you have to deal with increases, so does the likelihood of making the 'wrong' choice or making a mistake. Therefore, too much choice causes you to worry and to feel stressed, demotivated and anxious. In addition, we are constantly bombarded with adverts trying to sell us the next big thing, through many different platforms and media – it is overwhelming. Being presented with so many new daily choices again can lead to stress and anxiety.

So, if you identify with some of this, what should you do? Well, it will be difficult for a time but try to lower your expectations. Don't expect too much and you won't be disappointed. Although this may sound like a cliché, it is good advice for reducing stress. Try to settle for choices that are 'good enough', especially in the trivial areas of your life. And once you've made a choice, stop looking! Make a commitment to yourself that once you have made a choice, you'll stick with it rather than changing your mind if something better comes up. Thinking positively in this way will cause you less stress and help you to enjoy the choices you have made.

And then you can demonstrate one of the most crucial outcomes of positive thinking: being grateful.

CHAPTER 7

BENEFITS OF GRATITUDE

GRATITUDE

The British & Irish Lions is a rugby union team selected from players eligible from any of the home nations – England, Scotland, Wales and Ireland. The team plays every four years against Australia, New Zealand and South Africa in turn. For a professional rugby player, being selected for a Lions tour is a huge honour.

I know several rugby players who have played for the Lions and I am in awe of them when they share their experiences and what it means to them to be a Lion. In the rugby clubhouses across the UK and the Republic of Ireland, these players are seen as heroes and legends. That is why I was shocked to hear about the former British and Irish Lion, Gareth Thomas, being attacked one Saturday night in Cardiff. In a distinguished career, Thomas made over 100 test appearances for his country, played three tests for the Lions and captained both Wales and the Lions. In 2009, Thomas announced he was gay, becoming the first professional rugby union player to do so. I was particularly shocked to read that his attack was a homophobic attack.

However, the rugby world and the general public have been fantastic in their support of Thomas. The universal symbol for LGBT (lesbian, gay, bisexual, transgender) identity is a rainbow, and the weekend after Thomas had been attacked, a number of high-profile gestures using the rainbow symbol were initiated. These included the Welsh, French, US and the New Zealand (All Blacks) teams using rainbow-coloured laces to tie their boots. The US team posted on their Twitter feed, "We believe in rugby for all. Together, we stand with you." The French team posted, "We're all in with you on this matter." And the All Blacks posted, "All Blacks players will show their support for former Wales captain Gareth Thomas by wearing rainbow laces in their match against Italy tomorrow."

The support for Thomas has been wonderful and the condemnation of homophobia emphatic. Thomas was moved and humbled. That weekend he posted, "I wish I could put in words what this means." And those ten words that Thomas tweeted highlight another part of positive thinking – **gratitude**.

While the shock and sadness that Thomas experienced after the attack was significant, it was the support that he gained from so many quarters that helped him to start to recover in a positive way. By showing gratitude, and acknowledging it publicly, he was thinking positively about the attack. He could have been consumed with anger or regret, but once Thomas could see how many people were supportive, he was filled with gratitude, and that is such an important part of thinking positively.

GRATEFUL
LIVING

There is growing evidence that showing and experiencing gratitude can make you more determined, enthusiastic, energetic and optimistic. Robert A. Emmons, Professor of Psychology at the University of California, Berkeley, is the world's leading expert on gratitude. The research that Emmons and his colleagues have done suggests that gratitude can bring happiness. Gratitude has positive health implications by strengthening the immune system, lowering blood pressure and enabling better sleep. It can reduce anxiety and depression. It strengthens the belief that life is meaningful and manageable. Gratitude has a very powerful and lasting effect in that it can help reframe experiences in a positive way.

Gratitude is associated with how satisfied you are in life. The greater your gratitude the happier you'll feel. Those people who have a grateful nature are more likely to be happy.

In the brilliant TED Talk, "Want to be happy? Be grateful", viewed well over 6.8 million times, Benedictine monk David Steindl-Rast explains that happiness does not make us grateful, but it is gratefulness that makes us happy. He explains how there are people who seem to have everything – money, big houses, holiday home, expensive cars. But some of these individuals are still not happy because they constantly want more. Conversely, there are people who have had big setbacks and difficult experiences in their lives, but they seem very happy and contented. That is, in part, because they are grateful.

According to Steindl-Rast, when given a real gift, a gift that you have not bought, earned nor worked for, but that you see as valuable, the natural response is to show gratitude. Going back to Thomas the rugby player, the 'gift' he received from people publicly showing their support for him was a real gift. He did not ask for their support, he did not demand it; these people gave it freely. And with his tweet – "I wish I could put in words what this means" – he is demonstrating pure gratitude.

"WANT TO BE HAPPY?
BE GRATEFUL."

David Steindl-Rast

———

CULTIVATING GRATITUDE

With so many benefits that can be gained by being grateful, I recommend that you regularly try to do these three scientifically proven activities to help cultivate a gratitude mindset.

Every day, for at least a week, write down three things that went well and explain why. It is important to create a physical record of your list by writing it down, whether on paper or on a computer. It could be a small 'thing', like receiving a positive email that you were not expecting, or something more significant, like securing a new job. This practice will help you develop a more positive life outlook. You are retraining your brain to start focusing more on the good events that occur in your life, pushing negative feelings and disappointments to the side.

Write and send a letter or a card (not an email) to someone who has done something you are extremely grateful for. It could be a colleague, a friend, a family member or a stranger. In your writing try to reflect on what this person has done, how it affected you and why you are grateful. Writing a letter helps to express gratitude in a deliberate and thoughtful way to someone you have never properly thanked. This affirms how other people actually value and care for you.

Make time once a week to think about a significant positive event in your life. It could have happened last week or five years ago. Initially focus on the circumstances that made the positive event possible. Then consider the ways that this positive event might not have happened. Write down the possible decisions and events that could have led to a different outcome, which would have prevented this event from ever occurring. Visualize what your life would be like now if that positive event had not happened. Finally, shift your thinking to the fact that this positive event did indeed happen and the benefits you gained from it. Appreciate that these benefits were not guaranteed to happen in your life and allow yourself to feel grateful that things unfolded as they did.

These three activities will help you to appreciate what you already have in your life. By visualizing what your life would be like without them you will feel grateful about how things have turned out.

Research on gratitude also shows that people who have a grateful disposition are less envious, anxious, materialistic, depressed and lonely. It is one of the most important things associated with being satisfied with your life. It is a core part of positive thinking and you will gain so many benefits from embracing and practising gratitude.

As discussed in the introduction, a problem with the positive thinking movement of the last 75 years is that sometimes it has focused on deceiving yourself by denying the realities of your life. But as you will see in the next three chapters, embracing negative events, failure and challenging situations in a positive way can help you manage and get through them.

CHAPTER 8

COPING WITH DIFFICULT ISSUES

In 2016 Bruce Springsteen published his autobiography, *Born to Run*. I really like The Boss. I have five LPs in my vinyl collection, four albums on my phone and a video of one of his live shows. But until his autobiography, I only really knew about his music and nothing about him as a person. Up to that point, based on how he portrayed himself on stage, I had assumed that he was a happy, contented and successful musician. But, in reality only one of my assumptions was correct – he is an incredibly successful musician. The other two could not be farther from the truth.

According to his autobiography, as a child he was an "insecure, weird and skinny white boy" teased about a nervous tic. In school he was bullied and regularly upended into a rubbish bin. All of which seems light years away from his muscular onstage persona and powerful musical performances.

But the biggest surprise was about the fragility of his mental health. Springsteen revealed that throughout his adult life, he has suffered significant bouts of depression for which he has had to take antidepressants. He told *Sunday Times* journalist Nick Rufford: "Depression will steal your life. It will take it right out from underneath you by the things you do. You're under its sway. So psychopharmacology, for me and for my father, was very, very helpful."

The image of mental illness taking Springsteen's life from under him is a powerful one. When he is faced with anxieties and repeated bouts of depression, he feels like life is slipping through his fingers. As Springsteen highlights so well in his book, yes, there have been really positive things in his life, but also extremely difficult times, where the depression floored him. But rather than trying to deny that he was depressed or trying to block out all the negative thoughts that were consuming him, he faced up to the depression and sought help.

This is precisely the type of 'positive thinking' that I am advocating in this book, and Springsteen is a perfect example.

THE PARADOX

Think positively about **negative** things. This seems like a paradox, but that is one way to get through difficult challenges and situations. Positive thinking allows you to start thinking about how you could cope with difficulty rather than just pretending that it doesn't exist. Then you can prepare strategies and action plans to help you cope. Positive thinking doesn't mean that you bury your head in the sand and ignore life's less pleasant situations. Positive thinking means that you approach your problems in a more positive and productive way.

When facing an event or situation the first step is often self-talk. Self-talk is the endless stream of unspoken thoughts that run through your head. These automatic thoughts can be positive or negative. Some of your self-talk comes from logic and reason, or it may arise from misconceptions and misunderstandings. If the thoughts that run through your head are mostly negative, your outlook on life is more likely to be pessimistic.

Some common forms of negative self-talk include:

- Magnifying the negative aspects of a situation and filtering the positive ones. For example, you had a great day at work. You completed your tasks ahead of time and were complimented for doing a speedy and thorough job. But you had one conversation with a colleague that seemed negative and when you get home that evening that is all that you focus on and think about.

- When something bad occurs, you automatically blame yourself. For example, you hear that an evening out with friends is cancelled and you assume that the change in plans is because no one wanted to be around you.

- You automatically anticipate the worst. Out of the blue, your boss emails you, asking you to meet her at the end of the day and you automatically think that you are in trouble.

- There is no middle ground. You see things only as either good or bad.

If you suffer from some of these behaviours, here are some simple but effective ways to deal with them in a positive and constructive way:

Recognize your negative thoughts

Many of your thoughts are automatic. They just pop into your head without any conscious effort. So, be aware of your thoughts and evaluate them so you can recognize thoughts that are unrealistic, unproductive or irrational.

Look for evidence that your thought is true

Just because you think something doesn't make it true. In fact, most of your thoughts are likely to be opinions rather than facts. So, ask yourself, "What's the evidence that this is true?" Create a list of the evidence that supports your thoughts.

Look for the evidence that your thought isn't true

Now, create a list of reasons why your thought might not be true. If you struggle to find contrary evidence – which is common when your emotions run high – ask yourself, "What would I say to a friend who had this problem?" Give yourself the same consolation that you'd give someone else.

Reframe your thoughts into something more realistic

Once you've looked at the evidence on both sides of the equation, develop a more realistic statement. This is a very simple but effective way to start challenging some of the misconceptions and misunderstandings you may have about events that you have to deal with.

However, I am the first to acknowledge that managing and coping with negative emotions is very difficult and you probably won't be able to do it on your own. If you are suffering from conditions like stress, anxiety or depression you should discuss these with your doctor, a therapist, a counsellor or a spiritual advisor.

POSITIVE THINKING
MEANS THAT YOU
APPROACH YOUR
PROBLEMS IN A
MORE POSITIVE AND
PRODUCTIVE WAY.

——

A PERSONAL
EXAMPLE

I think it will be helpful to share my story about some of the mental health challenges I have faced, and how making the positive decision to seek help was crucial for managing my anxiety, which was, at times, debilitating.

For most of my life, I have suffered from anxiety. Sometimes it is mild, other times very significant. In my twenties and thirties, in the main, I tried to either ignore it or manage it myself. Then, after my stroke, for many years my anxiety was debilitating. I would go to my doctor regularly worried about a wide range of health issues – some justified, others not. This was how my anxiety manifested itself – it would latch onto a health worry that would spin 'round and 'round in my mind until I saw my doctor. In the short term seeing my doctor helped, but as soon as I read an article in a newspaper or watched TV programme about a health condition, my mind would then go into overdrive thinking that I had this particular illness.

With help, I realized that I was suffering from health anxiety. Once I knew its name, I could find ways to cope with it and manage it. This was when I made the positive decision to accept my health anxiety and put strategies in place to live with it. It took me about eight months from the point I thought I was going to have a mental breakdown to having the effective strategies that are still working today to help me cope. I know what the triggers are that could kick it off again, and one day it might happen again, but I accept that and I will be able to manage it if and when it does.

And sharing this very personal story, I think, allows me to be a very strong advocate of a different type of positive thinking. Suffering from a stroke and health anxiety, I have found that the emotional impacts are real, very difficult to cope with and incredibly challenging, not only to me but to all around me. However, by thinking positively and creating coping strategies, I can now finally see that good things have come from adverse events in my life and I am doing things now that once I would not have thought possible.

So, if you relate to some, or all, of this, be encouraged and think positively about the negative things in your life.

CHAPTER 9

THE GOOD THINGS ABOUT FAILURE

OK, let's talk about **failure**.

The topic of failure may not seem to fit naturally into a book about positive thinking. However, thinking positively about failure can fundamentally change how you can accept it and cope with it. And a great way to start talking about failure is to look at one of the most innovative thinkers of our times, Steve Jobs.

Jobs epitomized the daring and creativity of the tech industry's pioneering entrepreneurs. His passion and drive for innovation and immaculate design is well documented. As CEO of Apple, Jobs created one of the most valuable and admired companies in the world. And, along with it, a series of amazing products including the Apple Mac, iPod and iPhone. But before he led Apple to phenomenal success, Jobs experienced a number of significant failures.

At the start of the 1980s, Jobs was under pressure from his board to develop another breakthrough product, like the Apple I and the Apple II personal computers had been. So, first, in 1980, the Apple III was launched. However, unlike its predecessors, this model was an absolute disaster; it had an insane price of $4,340 and was prone to catastrophic overheating.

Then, in 1983 he launched the Lisa, a computer developed for business. Jobs was intent on making Lisa accessible to individual users rather than just focusing on business users. But the Lisa was as much of a failure as the Apple III. Then, in 1984, the company released the Macintosh (Mac). While it was initially celebrated by the media for its beautiful graphics, it turned out to be too underpowered to be truly useful and Apple struggled to sell the Mac profitably.

Such a stream of failures meant serious trouble for Jobs, and in 1985 the board sacked him from the company he had co-founded back in 1976. Being pushed out of the company he had worked so hard to grow into a recognizable brand was an incredible failure for Jobs. He admitted in 2005 that, "What had been the focus of my entire adult life was gone. It was devastating."

However, in 1986 Jobs invested in Pixar Animation Studios, an American computer animation film company. In 1995, Pixar partnered with Disney to produce its first animated film, *Toy Story*, which went on to be a huge box office success. This masterstroke also coincided with Pixar's initial public offering, making Jobs, who owned 80% of the company's shares, a billionaire overnight.

Apple began to really struggle in the 1990s and Jobs returned to take up the role of CEO again. He turned Apple's fortunes around with some fantastic and innovative products, such as: the far more powerful Mac, which redefined how personal computers function; the iPod, which completely revolutionized the music industry; and the iPhone, which has been equally important in the evolution of smart mobile phones.

In 2005, Jobs, himself a college dropout, shared the three most important stories from his life as he gave the commencement address at the prestigious Stanford University. One of these stories was about failure and how important it is to become successful.

"I didn't see it then, but it turned out that getting fired from Apple was the best thing that could have ever happened to me. The heaviness of being successful was replaced by the lightness of being a beginner again, less sure about everything. It freed me to enter one of the most creative periods of my life."

The lesson, it seems, is fairly simple. Even the great business visionaries and luminaries of our times experience setbacks and failure. Jobs suffered professional rejection, career setbacks and a debilitating blow to his self-confidence, but he managed to accept his failures, see the good things that had come out of them and, crucially, to learn from them to attain spectacular success.

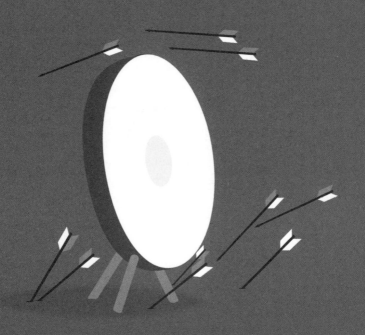

THE BENEFITS
OF FAILURE

And that is why failure and positive thinking can go hand-in-hand. Failure is a word associated with negative connotations that are often linked to fear and anxiety. This is a shame, because failure itself has unlimited potential to help us grow. It is through failure and making mistakes that we can discover novel and creative ideas. Take the light bulb, for example, developed by Thomas Edison, who is often credited with saying, "I have not failed 10,000 times – I've successfully found 10,000 ways that will not work." This illustrates the power of failure beautifully, and how to think positively about it.

Failure leads you to pursue more creative solutions. Accepting failure helps build resilience, which is important because success rarely happens on the first attempt. It is a very painful process you go through when you fail – your pride and self-confidence are normally hit hard. So, while it takes courage and self-belief to pick yourself back up after a failure, it is your resilience that keeps you moving forward, to keep on trying. Resilience will often ground you in reality, helping you to realize that success won't happen overnight but will take hard work and effort.

People who accept failure do not see it as a reflection on themselves but rather a reflection of the process they have gone through. When things do not go according to plan, they are better able to bounce back and try an alternative way of doing things. The experience and knowledge you gain when you encounter failure can be harnessed in the future to help you succeed in the long term.

Failure also helps you grow and mature. It helps you to challenge your purpose and beliefs about what you are trying to achieve. This helps you to reflect and put things into perspective, developing meaning from the painful situations that you experience. As long as you can identify why you failed, failure can be a brilliant teacher and help you not to make the same mistakes again.

Finally, failure also teaches you to value your success. If you have gone through periods of failure, then when success comes you will not take it for granted. You will feel that you have earned your success, when you reflect on the dark days when nothing seemed to be going right. There is nothing better than achieving success if you have gone through periods of failure to get there.

"I HAVE NOT FAILED
10,000 TIMES – I'VE
SUCCESSFULLY FOUND
10,000 WAYS THAT
WILL NOT WORK."

Thomas Edison

TESTED BY
ADVERSITY

One person who thinks positively about failure is the author of the Harry Potter series, J.K. Rowling. Rowling is one of the most inspirational success stories of our time. Many people probably know her simply as the creator of Harry Potter. But what most people don't know is that she experienced many years of failure and struggle before she achieved worldwide fame and success.

Back in 1990, Rowling first had the idea for Harry Potter. She has often told how the idea came fully formed into her mind one day while she was on a train from Manchester to London. She began writing furiously. In 1993 her first marriage ended in divorce, so she moved to Edinburgh, to be closer to her sister. In her suitcase were three chapters of Harry Potter.

Rowling saw herself as a failure at this time. She was jobless, divorced and penniless with a dependent child. She suffered from bouts of depression and eventually had to sign up for government welfare. It was a difficult time in her life, but she pushed through the setbacks, continuing to write, using the coffee shops of Edinburgh as her base.

In 1995, she sent the manuscript of her first Harry Potter book to 12 major publishers. They all rejected it. But she continued to believe that a publisher would pick it up. And one did – later that year, Bloomsbury accepted it and extended her a very small £1,500 advance. In 1997, the book was published with a print run of only 1,000 copies, 500 of which were distributed to libraries. In 1997 and 1998, the book won the Nestlé Smarties Book Prize and the British Book Awards' 'Children's Book of the Year'. After all that failure, Rowling had an explosion of success. Today, she has sold more than 400 million copies of her Harry Potter books and is the most successful female author in the UK. She has achieved worldwide recognition.

In 2008, Rowling was asked to give the commencement speech at Harvard University. It was a brilliant speech and a big part of it was about her experiences of failure: "The knowledge that you have emerged wiser and stronger from setbacks means that you are, ever after, secure in your ability to survive. You will never truly know yourself, or the strength of your relationships, until both have been tested by adversity. Such knowledge is a true gift, for all that it is painfully won, and it has been worth more than any qualification I ever earned."

So take a leaf out of the book of one of the most successful authors in the world and embrace failure. Think about and reflect on all the positive things that have come from all the setbacks and challenges you have overcome. Whatever form success takes when it eventually arrives, you will be wiser, stronger, more grateful and much more resilient.

You might be thinking, that all sounds fine but how do you actually make yourself more resilient? Well, you are about to meet one of the most extraordinary and brave young women I have ever known, who will show you.

CHAPTER 10

INCREASE YOUR RESILIENCE

RESILIENCE

I would like to introduce you to Becca, the girl who has no heart. I know of Becca because her dad, Michael, was a close school friend of mine and we have stayed in touch over the years.

To be clear, I am not suggesting that Becca has no empathy, love or kindness. In fact, she is the complete opposite. But Becca really has no heart! At the age of 23, she was diagnosed with a rare form of heart cancer. The doctors tried to treat the cancer with chemotherapy and radiotherapy, but to no avail. The only path left to save Becca was for the doctors to remove her heart. And that is what they did.

But Becca did not receive a transplanted biological heart. Instead, she has a Total Artificial Heart, which is a life-supporting cardiac system based on an external mechanical driver, with tubes that go into her abdomen. And she carries all of this in a rucksack on her back. This keeps her alive while she is waiting for a suitable heart donor. But even with all of that going in her life, Becca is still full of optimism and hope.

This whole story is amazing. I marvel at Becca's bravery, attitude and outlook on life. I admire the doctors' extraordinary skills that have kept Becca alive. When I see a Facebook update from her sitting in a restaurant or playing with her dog in the garden, it still blows my mind that she actually has no heart!

You see, I had assumed that it was impossible for anyone to live without a heart. However, when Becca was diagnosed with cancer, she posted regular Facebook updates on her progress. When she became very ill and was in intensive care, her parents kept the updates coming. Hundreds of her family and friends were able to find out how things were progressing for Becca. Then she went through the operation to remove her heart and, over many months, made a fantastic recovery. And then she started to do the Facebook updates herself again. And I saw all the things she was doing with her life. She has become an inspiration for many people.

And through all of this she has demonstrated incredible **resilience**, bouncing back after each setback. She is such a positive person and her resilience has contributed to this. Don't get me wrong, there were Facebook posts where Becca was very down, frustrated, angry or just sad, but each time she dusted herself off and bounced back.

If any statement sums up how resilient Becca is, then it is this from a Facebook update that she recently shared:

"YA GIRL IS IN REMISSION.

"Today got the results of my PET-CT scan and I'm officially cancer free; next one in six months. I may not have an actual heart anymore, but I also don't have cancer."

Six months later Becca announced that the hospital informed her that she was officially in remission.

ADVERSE EVENTS AND EXPERIENCES

Everyone faces difficult experiences and suffers adversity. But the key is how some people, like Becca, survive and thrive through these experiences whereas others give up and refuse to try again following the slightest setback.

I am a firm believer that positive thinking involves accepting challenging situations, but it is your resilience that helps determine if you will get through them or not. Since resilience contributes to your wellbeing and happiness – by allowing you to live a more rewarding life – it is key to thinking positively. Resilience also helps you to cope with stress in a positive way and is associated with longevity, lower rates of depression and having a greater satisfaction with life. Resilience will help you feel more in control. Likewise, a lack of resilience can mean that you may not handle the stress of difficult situations well. Chronic stress is associated with harmful health consequences such as high blood pressure, a weakened immune system, anxiety, depression, insomnia, heartburn, indigestion and heart disease.

There is growing evidence to suggest that resilience can be learned. For example, in 2008 the US Army was becoming increasingly concerned about the effects of multiple deployments on soldiers due to persistent conflicts. So, instead of focusing on treatments to combat conditions like post-traumatic stress disorder (PTSD), the US Army decided to be proactive and develop a way to increase the individual soldier's resilience before they faced traumatic situations. Comprehensive Soldier Fitness Resilience Training was created to give soldiers the life skills they needed to better cope with adversity and bounce back stronger from trauma.

Basically, its aim was to make soldiers more resilient. Since the Army rolled out the programme, four scientific and technical reports have been commissioned. The highlight of these studies is that soldiers who received the training reported higher levels of resilience and psychological health over time than soldiers who had not received it. The studies also showed that among those soldiers who had received the training, there were fewer diagnosed cases of anxiety, depression and PTSD.

But you don't need to enlist in the US Army to learn to be more resilient! There are some straightforward ways to do it! I will explain what those ways are, but first let me highlight some of the benefits of being resilient and how important it is to positive thinking.

People who demonstrate resilience are:

- more likely to see difficult situations, events and setbacks as manageable

- far more energized and driven

- better at coping not only with daily hassles but also with major challenges

- less emotional and more stable in their thinking

- usually optimistic about their future, and that optimism rubs off on the people around them

- more curious and open to new experiences

- more likely to accept personal responsibility for change rather than looking to others to fix things

DEVELOPING A MORE
RESILIENT YOU

Developing resilience is a personal journey, with people reacting in different ways to the same stressful life events. However, the American Psychological Association suggests trying some of these ideas to help you become more resilient:

Make connections
Good relationships with close family members, friends or others are important. Accepting help and support from those who care about you strengthens resilience. Assisting others in their time of need also can benefit the helper.

Avoid seeing crises as insurmountable problems
You can't change the fact that highly stressful events happen, but you can change how you interpret and respond to these events. Try looking beyond the present to how future circumstances may improve. Make a note of any subtle ways in which you might already feel better as you deal with difficult situations.

Accept that change is a part of living

Certain goals may no longer be attainable as a result of adverse situations. Accepting the circumstances that cannot be changed can help you focus on the circumstances you *can* change.

Move toward your goals

Develop some realistic goals. Do something frequently – even if it seems like a small accomplishment – that enables you to move toward your goals. Instead of focusing on tasks that seem unachievable, ask yourself, "What's one thing I know I can accomplish today that helps me move in the direction I want to go?"

Take decisive actions

Act on adverse situations as much as you can. Take decisive actions, rather than detaching completely from problems and wishing they would just go away.

Nurture a positive view of yourself

Developing confidence in your ability to solve problems and trusting your instincts helps build resilience.

Keep things in perspective

Even when facing painful events, consider the stressful situation in a broader context and keep a long-term perspective. Avoid blowing the event out of proportion.

Keep a resilience diary

Some people write about their deepest thoughts and feelings related to stressful events in their life. This helps because writing requires you to structure and organize your thoughts carefully and process the negative emotions that accompanied that stressful event.

Take care of yourself

Pay attention to your own needs and feelings. Engage in activities that you enjoy and find relaxing. Exercise regularly. Taking care of yourself helps to keep your mind and body primed to deal with situations that require resilience.

You may be comfortable with some of the above suggestions; others, not so much. The important thing is that you find what works for you and then get into the habit of doing it, or them, regularly and frequently. This will ultimately help you to become a more resilient person.

And remember Becca's inspirational story of resilience and positivity. She demonstrates so well why having a resilient mindset is such an important part of positive thinking to get through adverse events and situations.

The themes of acceptance, purpose, mindset, optimism, strengths, choice, gratitude, negativity, failure and resilience have helped me to rethink what it means to think positively. It is now time to have a history lesson that will illustrate perfectly how to start opening yourself up to new possibilities.

PART 2

OPENING YOURSELF UP TO NEW POSSIBILITIES

CHAPTER 11

WEARING YOUR VALUES

VALUES

One of the amazing things about being a father is watching your kids learn, develop and grow. When they are young, you are the teacher: imparting information, reading books, helping with school projects. When they are older, the roles sometimes reverse, and now it's me who is learning from them.

Let me show you a perfect example of this. My daughter, Lucy, is in her final year at Glasgow University, studying sociology. She recently sent me the introduction to her dissertation on homelessness. It was packed with detailed information, citations and case studies, much of which was new to me. And over the last four years, through Lucy I have learned so much new and fascinating information about various areas of sociology.

The area that Lucy is most passionate about, and has the most knowledge of, is women's rights.

Because of her I now have a far better understanding of the injustices and discrimination women have suffered for centuries. I know that today, all over the world, there are still women who have to fight for equal opportunities and rights. I also recently learned about International Women's Day, which was started in 1911 by the Suffragettes. When researching this on the internet I found the International Women's Day website and discovered a whole new and inspiring world. Quoting from the site, "International Women's Day means different things to different people, but the global focus on equality and celebration is clear. Throughout ancient and modern history, women have collaborated and led purposeful action to redress inequality in the hope of a better future for their communities, children and themselves. Whether through bold well-documented action or through humble resistance that never made it into the history books, women have united for equality and achievement forever."

International Women's Day is a particularly powerful collaboration led by the formation of a globally united movement for women, across countries, to come together. It has become a powerful global platform that unifies women and drives action for gender parity, while at the same time celebrating the social, cultural, economic and political achievements of women.

Their values made the biggest impact on me as they provided direction for the action, behaviour and ethos associated with this day, as well as for the work they do throughout the year that underpins the day itself.

The ten values that guide International Women's Day are:

justice	tenacity
dignity	appreciation
hope	respect
equality	empathy
collaboration	forgiveness

These values provide strong foundations for the work that gives positive outcomes every day for millions of women all over the world. And to me that shows that the International Women's Day organization is a positive thinking one. All the people (both women and men) organizing that day – and all the activities, campaigns and actions throughout the year – are thinking positively about how to achieve gender parity. And their values underpin their work and help them to think and act positively on narrowing the gap between the rights of women and men. By adhering to their values, they have a direction and a purpose in what they are trying to achieve.

International Women's Day has become the catalyst for so many positive outcomes for women, though as a society we still have a long way to go before we can truly say that men and women are treated equally.

VALUES AND
POSSIBILITIES

The people behind International Women's Day have identified values that give them purpose and direction. In a
similar way, when you are presented with a new possibility,
you need identifiable values that will guide you on whether
the possibility is one that you should pursue.

So, think about what values are important to you. Would
you pursue a possibility if it did not tally with your values?
For example, you see an interesting job vacancy posted,
but before you apply you visit the company's website and
discover that the company trades with countries whose pol-
itics and practices compromise your values. At this point
you need to make the decision about whether to apply for
the job or not, however interesting it seems.

Your values are important in the way you live and work.
They should determine your priorities, what you will spend
your time on and how you will engage with people. So,
when a possibility presents itself, investigate it further to
ensure that your values would not be compromised. It is up
to you whether you decide to pursue it further or walk away.

However, if you don't really know what your values are
or what you stand for, then the chances are that when a
possibility presents itself you will have no idea if it could
be a potentially positive or negative one. The consequence
of this is that you will be constantly struggling to decide

what you should focus your efforts on when new possibilities arise. So, rather than having your values guide you, you stumble between investigating each new possibility, without knowing which would be the right one for you. Procrastination and frustration lead to stress and anxiety. This is why it is important to identify your values: they provide direction for the possibilities you should pursue.

Having defined values is like writing an autobiography or making a brilliant film about your own life in reverse – you start with the ending! Imagine you're writing the last few sentences in your autobiography, closing with the words, "Finally, throughout everything I ended up pursuing in my life, it was sticking to my values that allowed me to achieve so many positive and beneficial things." What would those values be? Those values should be constant and should not really change throughout your life. They are what will drive you and keep you on the right path. Values are guiding principles that determine if you should act on a possibility or not.

IT IS IMPORTANT
TO IDENTIFY
YOUR VALUES;
THEY PROVIDE
DIRECTION FOR THE
POSSIBILITIES YOU
SHOULD PURSUE.

NELSON
MANDELA

In 2018, it was the 100th anniversary of the birth of Nelson Mandela, one of the most important figures of the 20th and 21st centuries. Known and loved around the world for his commitment to peace, negotiation and reconciliation, Mandela was South Africa's first democratically elected president (1994–1999), an anti-apartheid revolutionary and a politician.

To help celebrate this milestone centenary, the Nelson Mandela Foundation decided to revive the importance of values in society. The foundation was established in 1999 and one of its key aims is to promote dialogue around critical social issues, particularly issues regarding human rights and democracy, in order to contribute to a just society. The principles of the foundation come from the personal values that Mandela demonstrated throughout his life.

As part of the centennial celebrations, the foundation produced a t-shirt adorned with 240 words associated with Mandela's vision, wisdom and legacy. The words on the t-shirt form an illustration of his smiling face.

"Nelson Mandela was well known for attaching significance to what he wore," said foundation Chief Executive, Sello Hatang, at the launch of the t-shirt. The foundation had set an ambitious target to sell one million of the official t-shirts around the world, which in turn would help spread the values associated with South Africa's struggle to exchange apartheid for liberation. He stressed that proceeds from sales would go to helping the foundation continue Mandela's work.

"Every word on the t-shirt carries a value; it is a word you can take with you," said Hatang. "We want you to wear the t-shirt with a sense of pride in Mandela's legacy. We want you to pass on a message of a resilient nation, a caring nation."

People wore the t-shirts on 16 June, Mandela Day, and then on Mandela Fridays, which was a campaign to focus the attention of South Africans on deepening their democracy and realizing the dreams of Mandela.

It was a brilliant idea – wearing a t-shirt that demonstrates the values you support and believe in. In a similar way, you need to be constantly 'wearing' the values that are important to you. Everywhere you go, and whatever possibilities are presented, always 'wear' your values. These will guide and direct you on the ones you should pursue further.

Equally, when things get tough and you are really struggling to find the direction that you should take, 'wearing' your values can support and help you through difficult times. By sticking to your values at these times, you are thinking positively, and not compromising them, and you are likely not to pursue a possibility that, in the future, you might regret.

Millions of women, and millions of South Africans, have suffered so much over the centuries. But both groups have found that sticking to their values has helped them to achieve so many phenomenal things – things that both groups would once have thought impossible. Take a lesson from these two groups of people and just think that, by sticking with your values, what starts out as a mere possibility could turn out to be a life-changing experience for you.

USING YOUR IMAGINATION

The year is 1501. A sculptor is busy in his workshop, at the Piazza del Duomo, Florence. He is getting more and more frustrated trying to carve something from a massive block of marble. The marble had been quarried nearly 40 years earlier, in Carrara, Tuscany, for a series of sculptures (eventually abandoned) for Florence Cathedral. So, for 40 years, this block of marble lay unused. It had deteriorated and grown rough after years of exposure to the elements. As hard as he tries, he just cannot chisel the marble. In anger, he throws his chisel to the ground, gives up and walks away, muttering that nothing good could be created with this marble.

In a corner of the courtyard, a 26-year-old man was watching with interest as the sculptor got more and more irritated.

He smiled to himself when the sculptor finally gave up and stormed out of the courtyard. At last, he thought, I have found the slab of marble for the sculpture I have been commissioned to carve for Florence Cathedral.

The young man walked out of the courtyard and across of the Piazza del Duomo to the offices of the cathedral authorities. He explained that he could begin carving the marble to make the sculpture for the cathedral the next day. For him, the 'unworkable' block of marble was in fact the opposite.

By using only his imagination to visualize what this block of marble could eventually become, he could see a stunning and beautiful sculpture, not an unworkable block of marble. It was his job to discover the brilliant statue that hid inside it. What other sculptors thought impossible, this 26-year-old man thought completely possible.

This young man was Michelangelo, and his statue was eventually named David. Starting only with his imagination led him to carve one of the most famous works of art in the world. Michelangelo was quoted as saying, "Every block of stone has a statue inside it and it is the task of the sculptor to discover it."

So, what has this simple historical story got to do with positive thinking? Well, everything really, because using your imagination in a positive way will open up new possibilities.

You see, if you can't imagine what the possible might look like, there is no chance of you achieving it. Like the frustrated and the angry sculptor in the courtyard, who saw only an unworkable block of marble. In his mind, there was no possibility that anything good could be sculpted from it.

But Michelangelo thought differently. When he looked at the marble, he used his imagination to see, in his mind, a beautiful sculpture just waiting to be discovered. Where others saw impossibility, Michelangelo saw possibility. Unlike what the other sculptor saw as too much hard work, Michelangelo thought positively about what sculpture could be carved, even though he knew it would take him a considerable amount of time and effort.

But why did one sculptor see in his imagination a beautiful sculpture, where the other could imagine nothing good? Well, for most of his life Michelangelo had a voracious appetite for increasing his knowledge of the world he lived in. He was also incredibly curious and was fascinated by new things. These two things – knowledge and curiosity – are the bedrock of imagination.

THE 10,000-HOUR RULE

One of the benefits of living in a place like North Berwick is that it is only 25 miles from Edinburgh, Scotland's capital city. I am very fortunate that on my doorstep are stunning beaches, brilliant golf courses and a selection of great restaurants, shops, cafés and bars. Hop on the train at North Berwick, and within 30 minutes you are in the centre of Edinburgh – one of the world's great cities. Throughout the year, there are festivals, exhibitions, conferences and lectures by world-renowned speakers sharing their thoughts and ideas.

A couple of years ago, a good friend invited me to listen to one such speaker, Malcolm Gladwell, at one of Edinburgh's main theatres. Gladwell is a journalist for *The New Yorker* and a well-known author of five books, all of which have appeared in *The New York Times* bestseller list. The purpose of his talk that day was to share some of the ideas that appeared in his book, *Outliers: The Story of Success*. In *Outliers*, Gladwell examines the factors that contribute to high levels of success.

His talk was both inspiring and thought-provoking, in which he discussed the '10,000-hour rule', a key idea from his book. According to Gladwell, it takes 10,000 hours to achieve mastery over something and be successful at it. He uses The Beatles and Bill Gates as examples, to show that both were successful in their chosen fields, by dedicating at least 10,000 hours to either mastering the guitar and songwriting or understanding computer programming.

This sparked a thought in my mind about gaining knowledge to ignite imagination. Let's consider Bill Gates from a knowledge point of view. Whether he really dedicated 10,000 hours to understanding computing, I don't actually know. What I do know, however, is that from a young age Gates was fascinated with computers. In any spare time, he would either be learning about computers or programming. This is well documented in countless articles and books about him. And this led him to be incredibly knowledgeable about computing at a young age. It is the knowledge he accumulated during his youth that was crucial in allowing his imagination to envisage new possibilities about how computers could be used. By using that imagination, he became one of the world's greatest entrepreneurs and innovators, a visionary who has changed the face of computing forever.

"IT TAKES 10,000 HOURS TO ACHIEVE MASTERY OVER SOMETHING AND BE SUCCESSFUL AT IT."

Malcolm Gladwell
Journalist for *The New Yorker* and
a well-known author of five books

INCREASING YOUR
KNOWLEDGE

You see, without extending our knowledge, our ability to see things not as they are, but as they might be, is greatly hindered. If you cannot imagine new possibilities based on your current knowledge, your ability to think creatively is limited. How can you think of new ways to write a novel, compose a song or set up a new business if you keep coming back to existing and proven ideas?

So, to spark your imagination you need to increase your knowledge. Obviously reading is key, and it could be books, blogs, tweets, websites, Instagram, LinkedIn and Facebook posts – all will increase your knowledge. Rather than following subjects you are currently interested in, try following things that will challenge your current thinking. One tweet or post about something new could be the catalyst to spark your imagination about new possibilities in your life.

If reading is not your thing, then watch TED Talks, webcasts, documentaries and films, or listen to podcasts, radio programmes or audiobooks. Go to art galleries, museums, book festivals, bookshops, conferences and public seminars to get new ideas and perspectives.

By doing this you will challenge the status quo in your thinking, so that when you are presented with a new possibility your mind will not automatically revert to what you already know. In addition, if you can increase your knowledge on new subjects or further challenge or improve your current knowledge on something, then your imagination is more likely to see new possibilities.

REIGNITING YOUR CURIOSITY

So, increasing your knowledge is a key way to help you become more imaginative. The other way is to become more curious. Looking back to when my three children were very young, I can still remember the car journeys when they asked so many questions. Mealtimes were dominated by questions – questions about how things work, why certain things happen, where places are in the world. I have to say, it was exhausting! Children have a voracious appetite for learning about new things and are incredibly curious about the world around them. The more curious they become, the more imaginatively they think.

However, we get less curious as we become older. Many of us become fixed in our views and habits. Now and again we might watch a TV programme, like one of David Attenborough's documentaries, or read an article in a newspaper that makes us curious to find more out about the subject. But in the main we are creatures of habit, comfortable in what we already know. To help you become more imaginative you need to reignite that child-like curiosity you once had.

Let's go back to Michelangelo, who was one of the greatest artists who has ever lived and was known for his incredible work ethic. But what drove his work ethic was that he was curious about everything. He was a painter, sculptor, poet and architect, and not by chance. His profound interest in these disciplines led him to explore them until he decided to perfect the art of each.

There's a lesson you can learn from Michelangelo, and it's really quite simple – foster curiosity about ideas that have been sparked by accumulated knowledge. Start by asking basic questions about the idea. If you watch a TED Talk that inspires you with exciting thoughts, then go and find someone who could discuss it further with you. If you listen to a podcast that intrigues you, then find out more by posting questions focused on the subject of the podcast.

We tend to ask fewer questions as we get older. At some point in our process of growing up, questions start to be perceived by others as a weakness instead of a strength. However, if you want to open yourself up to new possibilities then I would urge you to resist that social pressure and continue to courageously ask questions, whether face-to-face or in cyberspace!

Study the lives of some of the world's greatest innovators, entrepreneurs, explorers, engineers, scientists, medics and artists and you will see that being curious is one of the key ingredients that made them successful. Alexander Fleming, Rosalind Franklin, Pablo Picasso, Marie Curie,

Leonardo da Vinci, Tracey Emin, Neil Armstrong and Florence Nightingale would have asked countless questions in their quest to achieve what they did in their lives. And I am certain that they would have asked loads of very basic questions on that journey!

I think that one of the most important benefits of being a more curious person is that you will become open-minded toward new ideas, interests and adventures. And this is when your imagination can really get to work!

So, constantly ask basic – even naive – questions, increase your knowledge wherever you can and become more curious about the world around you and you will create, or be presented with, new possibilities. Positive thinking is about you assessing which of these possibilities could become a reality. And one way to help you do this is to share!

CHAPTER 13

SHARING YOUR DREAMS

It's funny how things happen. Every morning, my wife and I walk our two golden retrievers and then we pop into our newsagent to buy a newspaper. However, this particular day the newsagent had sold out of the one we normally buy and there were only copies of *The Independent*. And that is how I came across an article that had a big impact on me.

That day, the *Independent* had a piece by journalist Sean O'Grady, in which he argued that one of the world's most famous speeches, Dr Martin Luther King Jr's "I have a dream", is the greatest speech of all time. Now, that is some claim, when you think of some other famous speeches. Think of Winston Churchill's "We will fight on the beaches"; Mahatma Gandhi's "Quit India"; Emmeline Pankhurt's

"Freedom or death"; John F. Kennedy's "The decision to go to the moon"; and William Wilberforce's "Abolition speech", to name just a few.

Well, to my shame, it made me realize that I had never read "I have a dream" in full. So, I downloaded a copy and read it, and after doing so I agreed with O'Grady – it really is a perfect speech. Everything was right about it; even the location on the steps of the Lincoln Memorial was an ideal setting, with its historical importance in the history of the United States. The Lincoln Memorial is a monument honouring the 16th president of the United States, Abraham Lincoln. King spoke to both the heads and the hearts of his audience, whether they were in the crowd or listening to the radio or watching TV. He used both vivid and metaphorical language to capture their attention. He reinforced key points through repetition, his call to action is clear and concise, and he ends on a hopeful note. More than 200,000 people attended the speech, creating an electric atmosphere.

But for me, there is another important aspect to his speech: it is about possibility. And how did King communicate this? He shared his **dream** with as many people as possible. For example, with "I have a dream that my four little children will one day live in a nation where they will not be judged by the color of their skin but by the content of their character", he shows what is possible.

BENEFITS FROM SHARING

Sharing dreams is important because doing so at the right time and with the right people can mean that those dreams are more likely to become genuine possibilities. It makes you accountable not only to yourself but also to those you have shared your dreams with. When you share a dream with someone, you make a promise to yourself to take positive action and make it a possibility. King's whole life was driven by this. Look what his speech did for the civil rights movement. People worldwide were motivated and galvanized to make equality possible for all, regardless of ethnicity, gender or religion.

By sharing your dreams you can get help from others. Whether it's with one person or thousands, by sharing with others you are more likely to make something a possibility. As long as you share your dream with the right people – people you trust or who have similar dreams to you – they are likely to want to help you make it possible.

Sharing can also keep you on track. People will regularly ask you how it's progressing, keeping it at the front of your mind and creating a brilliant 'progress board' that keeps you on target!

Let me illustrate what I mean by all of this by introducing you to one of my close friends, Steve, and the benefits he gained from sharing his dream with the right people and at the right time.

AS LONG AS YOU
SHARE YOUR
DREAM WITH THE
RIGHT PEOPLE,
THEY ARE LIKELY
TO WANT TO HELP
YOU MAKE
IT POSSIBLE.

YACHT
MAN

I have known Steve for well over 20 years. We have gone through a lot together, especially following my stroke, when he was very supportive. We have competed against each other in sports, sorted out the world's problems over too many beers in our local pub and worked together on projects.

About five years ago, Steve and his wife, Lynda, went on a sailing holiday in the Mediterranean. They both loved the whole experience, but for Steve it was the catalyst that helped him develop a dream that one day he and Lynda would buy a catamaran and sail around the world. But at that time his dream was not a possibility for four reasons. The first and most obvious one was that Steve could not sail. Second, they were not in a financial position to buy a catamaran. Third, Steve had recently been diagnosed with a heart condition which would require regular check-ups with his physician. And finally, but crucially, Lynda did not share the same dream as Steve!

But that sailing holiday in the Mediterranean had a big effect on him. To see if the dream of buying a catamaran could be a possibility, he shared his dream with his business partner, Andrew. Steve and Andrew had co-founded their business back in 2005, Lynchpin Analytics. That was the catalyst that started the discussions and led to a plan resulting in Lynchpin buying Steve's shares. They agreed upon a price in 2017, and on 30 March 2018 Steve officially retired from Lynchpin.

Steve continued to share his dream with anyone who asked him about what he was going to do when he retired. He received a balance of good – 'brilliant, go get that dream' – and bad reactions – 'it'll never happen'.

He told me recently: "The naysayers kept me on my toes. If they raised an issue that may have stopped or hindered my dream, I researched the issue to find a solution. Their negativity also pushed me to prove them wrong."

Through sharing, Steve also received information that would enable the possibility of sailing around the world. A friend who is a doctor advised him to visit his physician and discuss the health implications of long sailing trips. He also suggested some new medication which meant he did not need to be monitored frequently.

Then, a Lynchpin customer emailed him about a 14-week Yachtmaster course based in Gibraltar. The Yacht-master qualification is the ultimate aim of many skippers, both professional and recreational, as it covers everything you need to know about sailing. Steve booked himself into the course that started the day after he had officially retired.

The final and crucial point was that Lynda eventually came to share the same dream. "I suppose it was like osmo-sis. As I spoke about it to myself, her and other people she saw my desire, passion and reasoning and it slowly brought her 'round," Steve recalls.

Steve's dream was now a real possibility. He had the solu-tion to becoming a qualified yachtsman, the money to buy a yacht, the medication to allow him to sail wherever he wanted to go, and Lynda now also had the same dream.

The positive outcome of all of this was that in March 2019, Steve and Lynda purchased a catamaran and they set out from Gibraltar to sail around the Mediterranean.

All because Steve shared his dream at the right time and with the right people.

INTELLIGENT RISKS

So, here we have two examples of the power of sharing your dream. One from a man who helped society and left a legacy for the world. The other from my good friend who is now doing things he thought would not be possible a few years ago. However, unlike King and Steve, there are many people for whom their dreams don't become a possibility.

How can a dream become a possibility? Well, it all boils down to risk and reward. I talked about this in my first book, *Changing Course*.

In my view there are two types of risks: **unwise risks** and **intelligent risks**.

- **Unwise risks**
  With these, your potential outcome is negative, and the potential upside is very limited.

- **Intelligent risks**
  With these, your potential outcome is positive, and the potential downside is very limited.

So, is sharing your dream with lots of people an unwise or an intelligent risk? Let's go back to Steve. At the start he only shared his dream with a limited number of people whom he trusted – his wife, his business partner Andrew and his doctor. Before then, if he had told everyone about his dream, in my opinion this would have been an unwise risk. There was little chance of it becoming a possibility and he probably would have been ridiculed, so there was no real upside in sharing it.

But slowly, as solutions started to appear that addressed the main obstacles in his way, he started to share his dream with a wider group. By doing that he was taking intelligent risks. The only downside was that there may have been other obstacles in the future that he had not yet thought of. The upside, though, was enormous, because he found solutions to all of the obstacles, more and more people wanted to help him, and he was encouraged and motivated by all the positive feedback. And the people who did not believe Steve could do it motivated him to prove them wrong. He was now accountable to himself to make sure it did happen. And his friends regularly kept asking him how he was progressing.

And that is how you discover new possibilities. Articulate in your own mind what that dream is. Then list the obstacles that you think are in the way. Finally, look at all the contacts you have and determine who can help you. If you trust them and value their views, then tell them about what you want to do. Trust me, it is as simple as that and it works. They might not have a solution straight away, but at some point they will either have one or put you in touch with someone who can help.

Now, I cannot guarantee that these new possibilities will one day become a reality. However, take intelligent risks when you share a dream and the new possibilities will start to appear.

So, three ways to open yourself up for new possibilities in your life – wear your values, use your imagination and share your dreams. But there is another way, and to show you what that is I want you to meet Brandon.

OPEN UP YOUR CREATIVE MIND

In my view, a book is one of the most thoughtful gifts you can give. Whether it's a crime thriller, fictional adventure, historical biography, self-help manual or something entirely different, a book has the power to spark curiosity, introduce innovation and open up new ways of thinking. It is a gift that says, "Hey, I read this book and I think you might like it" or "I read a review of this book and I think it is right up your street." It really is a great gift to give.

And so, when my daughter Lucy gave me a book as a Christmas present I was delighted with her choice. I ripped off the wrapping paper to find the book *Humans of New York*, by Brandon Stanton. What a choice! To quote from the blurb in the inside cover of the book, "In the summer of 2010, photographer Brandon Stanton set out on an ambitious project: to single-handedly create a photographic census of New York City. Armed with his camera, he began criss-crossing the city, covering thousands of miles on foot, all in an attempt to capture New Yorkers and their stories. The result of these efforts was a vibrant blog he called 'Humans of New York,' in which his photos were featured alongside quotes and anecdotes."

Published in 2013, this book was inspired by the content of Stanton's blog. It is a stunning collection of 400 colour photographs of the personalities in New York City. Not only do I think it is a brilliant idea for a book, it also shows how **creativity** can lead to new possibilities!

So, let me tell you a bit about Stanton and how he embraces possibility. Before 2010, Stanton had never owned a camera, but in January that year, at the age of 26, he decided to buy one. At that time he was working as a bond trader and could only take photos on weekends, in downtown Chicago where he lived. He would photograph anything that caught his attention – buildings, nature, people. As he said in the book, he fell in love with taking photos. "Photography felt like a treasure hunt, and even though I sucked at it, I'd occasionally stumble upon a diamond. And that was enough to keep me wanting more."

But what took Stanton from being a full-time bond trader to one of the most famous photographers in the world today? In 2010 he lost his job, which made him reassess what he wanted to do with his life. And he decided that he wanted to become a full-time photographer, even though he had little experience. So, although losing a job can be catastrophic for some, this event became the catalyst that changed Stanton's career and, subsequently, his life. When he was made redundant, the possibility of becoming a full-time photographer opened up.

By focusing all of his time on photography he was able to nurture his creativity. Not only did he continue to take a variety of photographs, he also moved to a new city, Philadelphia, and started doing the same there. After Philadelphia he decided to move to New York and that was when his creativity exploded. What fascinated him was not the buildings or famous landmarks but the people. As he said, "The buildings were impressive, but what struck me most were the people. There were tons of them. And they all seemed to be in a hurry."

That was his inspiration to start an album for his New York photographs. He called it 'Humans of New York' and he took thousands of pictures. And that photo album became the book I received from Lucy at Christmas.

One of the major things that Stanton found out about himself was that once he was given the right environment, the right location and the right people, he could unleash his creativity. And this creativity opened up a new world of possibilities that eventually led him not only to publish *Humans of New York* but also *Humans of New York Stories* and *Little Humans*. In addition, his website shows he has also expanded to feature photos and stories from over 20 different countries.

So how easy is it to use your creativity to open up new possibilities?

UNLEASHING
YOUR CREATIVITY

If you look for 'how to be more creative' on the internet you will find website after website with lists of ideas, tips and tools. And that is all useful, but I want to focus on the main triggers that unleash your creativity. In my opinion there are three main triggers: right location, right environment and right people. Any or all of these will help you to be more creative.

Right location

Over the years I have attended many conferences and seminars all over the world, either as an attendee or as a speaker. Not only do I enjoy going to these events, but it also gives me the opportunity to visit new cities and places. And, looking back, I think my creativity increased when I found myself in new locations, as I always allowed a few days for sightseeing. For example, in Chicago I spent a weekend being a tourist and visited the Sears Tower, the Art Institute of Chicago, and an American football game and a baseball game. As much as I enjoyed these experiences, they also helped me relax, opened my mind and gave me the space to think. Often, I was inspired by the things

I experienced and would return home with new and exciting possibilities in my mind. When I came back from Chicago, I had an idea for a new part of the business, which subsequently became very successful. That new location of Chicago was the trigger for my creativity to help me open up my mind to new possibilities.

It is no coincidence that authors and artists visit retreats to help them become more creative. Likewise, companies organize team days away from the office, normally in hotels or unusual venues to help them shape a new strategy, away from the distractions of the normal working day. This, I believe, makes people more open-minded and relaxed, aiding creativity.

But you don't need to go to Chicago or move to New York to experience a new location! My guess is that there will be villages, towns and attractions, no more than an hour away, that you have never visited. When you are on holiday, rather than spending the whole week lying next to the pool, take one day and visit something you wouldn't normally. If you are attending a conference or a seminar, plan your trip to allow you at least half a day to sightsee.

Sooner or later, something will spark your creative mind to see or create new possibilities.

Right environment

Another great way to trigger your creativity is to work somewhere different on a regular basis. I don't mean all the time, but at least a few hours a week. Whatever you do, if you want to become more creative in your thinking then a great trigger to help you to do that is to find a new space to spend some time in.

So, if you have wanted to write a book, rather than doing it from your home you can go to a different environment. This might be your local library, or a museum or your favourite coffee shop. If you have just set up a new business and you are working from home, then join a shared office space. Most have starter packages where you can use the office for a few hours a week at a very reasonable cost. If you are in a profession like nursing or teaching, if at all possible stop somewhere new on your way home, such as a café, or take a walk for at least an hour.

What you are trying to do is to find a place that is not your home or your normal place of work, but somewhere you can really focus on your thinking to help you get the inspiration for your next chapter, solve a business challenge you are currently facing, or simply reflect on your day to see if you could have done anything differently.

Right people

If you have read any of my books, you'll have seen that there is a constant theme – I love writing stories about people. Some of these people I have worked with, or caddied for or known since childhood. Some are artists or sportspeople, or people I admire from history or in business. Some I have met face-to-face, others I have read about, or watched a TED Talk or a YouTube video that features them.

Whoever they are, and wherever I have encountered them, they have inspired me to such an extent that I want to share their stories in my books. This for me is always the start of the creative process for my chapters. I just love dipping into their lives, finding out a bit more about them. Often, something they have said, or their ideas and insights, sparks my own creativity.

Just meeting people can also be the trigger for your creativity. So, you might ask, how do I find the right people to meet? Not everyone wants to join a business club, a book club, a sports club, a networking event, a course, a conference, a seminar or an art event! If that is you, turn to the internet. There are so many fascinating and inspiring people you can 'meet' on Wikipedia, YouTube, blogs, Instagram, TED Talks, LinkedIn and Twitter, to name just a few.

Just read or watch or listen to their stories and you will be amazed how that will help you to become more creative. It has certainly worked for me!

So, back to Stanton. His books and all his social activity are hugely successful and that is because, in part, he let his creativity blossom by changing where he lived, altering his environment and meeting thousands of new people. I cannot guarantee that you will become as creative as Stanton, but if you try to find, every now and again, a new location or a new environment or new people, then your creativity will be awakened and new possibilities will emerge.

CHAPTER 15

IDENTIFYING YOUR GOALS

GOALS

My guess is that most people have had the 'who would you invite to dinner' conversation with family, friends or their partner. All you need to do is pick five people, past or present, to sit around your dinner table. So who would it be? It is an interesting conversation to have because, at its root, it shows those people who inspire you. My five invitations would go to Barack Obama, Billy Connolly, Tom Hanks, Fiona Bruce and Ed Stafford. I think most of you will have heard of the first four, but possibly not Ed Stafford.

Ed achieved the seemingly impossible – he walked the entire length of the Amazon River from its source in Peru to the sea in northeastern Brazil. Some 860 gruelling days, 9,000,000-odd steps, more than 200,000 mosquito and ant bites, about 600 wasp stings, six pairs of boots and a dozen scorpion stings later Ed completed the walk on 9 August 2010. For two and a half years he filmed and blogged about his challenging journey and engaged followers from all over the world. When he completed the walk, a film company commissioned a documentary using Ed's video footage. I vividly remember watching that documentary, *Walking the Amazon*, and being in total awe of what he had achieved.

This feat of endurance had a big impact on me. Not only was the walk an extremely difficult physical challenge, it was also an emotional rollercoaster! Along the way, he experienced not only despair, fear, exhaustion and sadness but also joy, laughter, happiness and elation. Sir Ranulph Fiennes described Ed's expedition as being "truly extraordinary … in the top league of expeditions past and present."

Since his epic journey, Ed has completed a number of other challenges where he has had to survive in very hostile environments. He has also written a number of books and made several documentaries about his experiences.

And so yesterday, as I was driving to Edinburgh, I was delighted to hear Ed being interviewed on BBC Radio 5 Live about his new book, *Adventures for a Lifetime*. The interview was fascinating. He talked about his new book, but the rest of the interview focused on his life and why he was motivated to challenge himself and explore the world. One comment stood out for me: "Putting yourself in situations where you don't necessarily have all the answers and where there probably is an element of danger involved, I think, if you put yourself in these situations in life they are really good for you and you grow and evolve as a person."

He sees adventures as a way to develop and grow in life. That is why he does them. He sees adventure as a way to find out more about himself and what motivates him. But what impressed me most was how he remained so positive that he could complete the challenge, and his belief that it would better him as a person. That was his **goal** and that was at the core of his motivation.

APPROACH AND AVOIDANCE GOALS

One aspect of thinking positively is that it helps you to set goals. There are two types of goals. The first are 'approach goals', which work toward positive (or desirable, pleasurable, beneficial and liked) outcomes. Ed's goal is an example of an 'approach goal' because he wanted to challenge himself to achieve a goal never before completed – to walk the complete length of the Amazon. The second type are 'avoidance goals'. These are negative (or painful, disliked, harmful and undesirable) goals because you will work hard to avoid a negative outcome. A good example of an avoidance goal could be to move out of the city because it is noisy and busy. Moving to a new house is one of the most stressful events you can undertake, as it is a long process, very costly, packed with uncertainties and with no guarantee that it will be a success.

If you want to use positive thinking to see if a possibility could be a realistic and achievable goal, then you should focus mainly on approach goals and try to sidestep avoidance goals. In fact, setting avoidance goals is a stressful process and the constant monitoring of negative possibilities drains your energy and enjoyment, which can lead to stress, anxiety and disappointment. However, setting approach goals and working toward achieving a possibility makes us feel good, and we get a sense of satisfaction and pleasure from identifying and pursuing them. All of this can make you more energized, contented and satisfied.

SPECIFIC   MEASURABLE   ACHIEVABLE   REALISTIC   TIME-BOUND

GOAL
SETTING

One of the best and most useful ways of setting and achieving both approach and avoidance goals is to use the SMART methodology. SMART stands for:

S pecific
Is your goal well defined and clear, and understood by everyone who is involved in achieving it?

M easurable
Is the goal obtainable and measurable, so you know when it has been achieved?

A chievable
Is the goal within your capabilities of achieving it?

R ealistic
Can you achieve the goal with your current resources and knowledge?

T ime-bound
Have you set a target date and allowed yourself sufficient time to achieve the goal?

If you apply the SMART methodology to goal setting, then you are more likely to achieve your goal.

Going back to Ed, his goal of walking the entire length of the Amazon used SMART. This helped him to stay motivated even when he was facing danger, encountering setbacks or was simply exhausted. Because his goal was specific, measurable, achievable, realistic and time-bound he achieved what, for most people, is a goal that would be impossible. So, whenever you are presented with a possibility, apply SMART to see if the possibility could be a goal that you want to pursue.

But what is really important in all the suggestions and ideas I have shared so far in this book is that if you want to open yourself up to new possibilities that could enhance your life, and benefit from thinking positively, then you really need to know who you are.

CHAPTER 16

EMBRACING WHO YOU ARE

I want to share with you an extraordinary and uplifting story about one of my neighbours, Rachel Woods. She really encapsulates what this chapter is all about – **identity**, and how powerful it can be for opening yourself up to new possibilities.

At the age of ten, Rachel was diagnosed with high-functioning autism. In the years before her diagnosis, her parents began to notice that she was developing in a different way from her two older sisters. When she started nursery and then primary school, the teachers saw that the way she communicated was slightly different from the other children. This was one of the things that led her doctor to refer Rachel to a local hospital, where a specialist in autism confirmed the diagnosis.

And over the 14 years since that diagnosis, with fantastic support from her family, the school, her friends, her work colleagues and health professionals, Rachel has gone on to achieve so much. She has accepted that she has autism and is fully aware of the challenges it brings to her life. Those challenges are mainly in the area of communication and being in unfamiliar social situations.

At school she achieved five Standard grades and three Highers and became a member of the Scottish National Girls' Choir. At the age of 17 she moved with her parents to New Zealand for three years. When the family moved back to Scotland, Rachel initially found it difficult to get a job. So, she volunteered at Oxfam and also at a local charity. At the same time, she went to Edinburgh College and graduated with an SVQ (Scottish Vocational Qualification) in Business Administration.

Again, she found it very difficult to get a job. She was successful in getting interviews but, frustratingly, the interview never culminated in a job offer. She commented many times to her parents that the companies who interviewed her seemed to identify her mostly as someone with a disability rather than a suitable candidate for the job.

But Rachel did not give up – she was motivated to prove that people with high-functioning autism could find employment. When talking to Rachel about where this motivation came from, she said that "85% of people with high-functioning autism don't get jobs but I don't want to be one of them."

And that motivation led her to apply for a modern apprenticeship at VisitScotland, Scotland's national tourism organization. This allowed Rachel to earn a wage and at the same time gain an industry-recognized qualification. From the outset, VisitScotland saw Rachel as someone who had all the attributes for a modern apprenticeship, rather than someone who had a disability. Based on that they offered Rachel a job.

That was three years ago and today Rachel is a valued member of the team. In fact, she has made such a positive contribution to the organization that in 2018 the marketing director at VisitScotland asked Rachel if he could recommend her to the TED organization to give a TED Talk. And TED were so impressed with Rachel's application that they invited her to give a TED Talk at the Scottish TED conference in June that year. Rachel accepted their invitation, and gave a talk with the title, "Let's rethink ability and autism".

Now, for someone with high-functioning autism to give a live talk to hundreds of people is quite remarkable. Rachel finds large groups of people incredibly daunting. She struggles, when stressed or anxious, to communicate well. She worries that when people look at her, they see someone who is slightly different. But even given all of these challenges, she was determined to deliver the speech.

And it is a brilliant speech. It lasts for about nine minutes and Rachel encapsulates what it means to live with autism. She is passionate about ability and autism but also angry about the lack of job opportunities for people with autism.

She communicates powerfully the positive benefits for employers in hiring someone with autism, such as super attention to detail, intense focus on tasks and excellent time-keeping skills. And she pleads with employers to look at the positive aspects of autism and not just see it as a barrier for someone to be successful in a business.

For me, the most important message from Rachel's speech is that she accepts who she is and, more importantly, that she sees being autistic as a part of her identity. As she said in her speech, "I get anxious telling people I have autism. But I should not hide it. Autism is a part of who I am. And the world needs to embrace it. Because I am part of this world too."

And that is why embracing your identity and being comfortable with it – as Rachel has done, and is – can open up a number of new possibilities in your life.

"LET'S RETHINK ABILITY AND AUTISM."

Rachel Woods

___

WHAT IS
YOUR IDENTITY?

Embracing your identity is important for seeing or creating possibilities because if you try to deny who you actually are it is very difficult to think positively and see new possibilities. When Rachel positively embraced the fact that she has autism and was happy to communicate that to everyone she met, new possibilities started to appear. The possibility that – with the right help and support – she could apply for a modern apprenticeship. Because she had impressed the marketing director at VisitScotland with her work ethic and her attitude, it became a possibility that he felt she could give a TED Talk and share her experiences. And the key here is that she thought about these possibilities, weighed up the risks of doing it (which were significant) and decided that she was capable of pursuing these as possibilities.

That was my experience, too. Once I had embraced the fact that I was a stroke survivor and that this was now a positive part of my identity, new possibilities in my life started to emerge.

People are mostly defined by what they do for a living. Just think back to the last time you were at a party and you met someone for the first time. I bet that within a few sentences of being introduced to them, the conversation got around to what you do for a living. Without knowing it, we all wear 'badges' that say 'this is me' to people you meet – I am a doctor or an IT director, or a mother of young children or a waiter. That is what 'identifies' you, this 'role badge'. The problem is that if you lose this identity, for example if you are made redundant, or have a serious health issue or your children leave home, then that badge no longer applies. Equally, the badge that you currently wear might be one that gives you little self-confidence, or something that you are not very proud of, so it may be that you don't like your current identity. Both of these scenarios – losing or not liking your identity – make it very difficult to open yourself up for new possibilities

So, if you are in a similar position as I was – initially not accepting that I was a stroke survivor – then take a leaf out of Rachel's book. Celebrate and embrace who you are, don't be embarrassed about it, and tell everyone because that is what a part of thinking positively is. And new possibilities will occur.

ACCEPTING
YOUR IDENTITY

By accepting who I am, numerous possibilities have opened up to me. Once I accepted that I was a stroke survivor and that it was OK, I started to try to find out about other stroke survivors and what they were doing with their lives. And boy, was I inspired by so many incredible stories! One that inspired and motivated me like no other was the story of Jean-Dominique Bauby, who until 1995 was the editor ofFrench *Elle* magazine. In his early forties and enjoying life with his young children, Jean suffered a massive stroke that left him completely incapacitated. Jean's stroke resulted in a phenomenon known as locked-in syndrome, in which the body and most of the facial muscles are paralysed but consciousness remains. The outcome for Jean was that he was left paralysed from the neck down, although he could swivel his head from side to side.

He worked with a speech therapist in the hope of finding a way to communicate. To help him, the therapist reordered the alphabet and developed a communication code especially for him. The code was based on the alphabet being organized according to each letter's frequency of use in the French language. Jean blinked his one working eyelid until he reached the letter desired and then started again for the next letter in a word. The process was incredibly laborious, but Jean was determined to write a book that covered his life before and after the stroke.

Jean's book, *The Diving-Bell and the Butterfly,* is a series of memories and brief visits to the hospital from people who have not classified him as a vegetable. There is no sense of self-pity or hopelessness in Jean's story. He quickly adjusts himself to his new life and works to make the best of it. Jean's story is one of great courage about still trying to live life to its fullest regardless of what has happened.

It also showed me that it was possible, even for someone who had had a horrific stroke, to write a beautiful and inspirational book. If it was a possibility for Jean, then, I thought, it was a possibility for me. Once that possibility had crystallized in my mind, I then started to weigh up how I could make this happen. In the ten years since I read Jean's book, I have now written three books. All of these books have been possible because I finally accepted my new identity.

So, like Rachel, Jean and me, embrace your identity, as it is one of the best ways to open yourself up to new possibilities. And whatever possibilities you decide to pursue, try to ensure that there is a very high chance that they will provide you with happiness, kindness, joy, hope, enthusiasm and inspiration. As you are about to see, the benefits of doing that are significant.

CHAPTER 17

THE OUTCOMES OF POSITIVE EMOTIONS

Call it coincidence, or something else, but this morning I was planning to write the final chapter. So, to get me in the right frame of mind for writing, I took my dogs out for a long walk along the beach, close to where I live. It was a stunning, clear, crisp winter's day. As I walked, I started to develop, in my mind, a structure for the chapter. I already knew the main points I wanted to make, and how I wanted to conclude not only this chapter, but the whole book. However, I was really struggling to find a relevant opening story for the final chapter, without which it wouldn't work.

I came off the beach and popped into our local news-agent to buy a copy of *The Times* newspaper. I returned home, made a coffee and sat down to read it. And then, on the front page, I read an article by Kat Lay, *The Times'* health correspondent, which I found so relevant and perfect for this last chapter. I was staggered!

Titled "Why positive thinking is the best way to get a grip", the article detailed a recent study by researchers from University College London that concluded that positive thinking can help your health, emotionally, physically and cognitively, in your later years.

The study, published in *Proceedings of the National Academy of Sciences* (*PNAS*), was conducted by Professor Andrew Steptoe. He and his team analysed data collated between 2012 and 2016 from more than 7,000 adults over the age of 50, as part of the English Longitudinal Study of Ageing (ELSA).

When asked 'to what extent they felt the things they did in their life were worthwhile', participants were instructed to rate their answer on a scale from one to ten. Researchers found that those who rated higher lived life significantly better. It showed that having a sense of purpose and feeling engaged in worthwhile activities may promote health and happiness in later life.

Professor Steptoe said, "As more and more men and women live longer, we need to understand better what factors lead to healthier and happier older age." He explained, "This is a two-way process. Not only do good social relationships and better health contribute to our sense that we are living meaningful lives, but this sense of meaning sustains social and cultural activity, health and wellbeing in the future."

Here, in the article, was the core purpose of this book – that is to say, that engaging in the right kind of positive thinking can be of benefit in so many physical and emotional ways.

POSITIVE
EMOTIONS

Everybody likes to feel good. It's one of the very few things I guess that all humans – of every race, colour, creed, religion, gender, sexuality and political persuasion – have in common. We all like to feel good, and positive emotions feel… well, feel good! There is now mounting scientific evidence that experiencing positive emotions like happiness, enthusiasm, joy, hope, kindness and inspiration are vital for living a happy and healthy life.

Positive emotions are not simply 'happy feelings' that we chase to feel momentary pleasure; positive emotions play a significant role in everyday life. While you will probably not achieve lasting meaning and happiness based on temporary, hedonistic pleasures alone, positive emotions often provide the foundation for those meaningful moments that make life worth living and make you happy. For example, think of the joy you get from your family or the immense satisfaction you get from achieving something great in your career.

There are many research studies that outline the benefits of positive emotions. For example, positive emotions are linked to many outcomes:

> living longer
> better quality relationships
> fully engaged in the things you do
> being more resilient and persistent
> better mental and physical health
> more creative in your thinking
> more effective decision-making

One of the most important questions on this subject is whether positive emotions are the cause or the effect of these outcomes. The evidence on this front is less extensive; however, there is growing evidence that, in many areas, positive emotions may lead to successful outcomes rather than just following on from them. As a result, it seems that positive emotions do lead to important outcomes, such as a feeling that your life is meaningful, having fulfilled and productive work, enjoying satisfying relationships, and experiencing better mental and physical health and longevity.

However, there is an important caveat to all of this. I don't want you to fall into the trap of thinking positive emotions are always good and negative emotions are bad, as this is simply not the case. All emotions, positive or negative, are normal. Negative emotions, such as being fearful about a potentially harmful situation, mean you get away from danger as quickly as you can. So, negative emotions are obviously very good for you for reasons of self-preservation, in this example. There are countless books and research articles on negative emotions such as fear, anger, sadness and guilt, but fewer on positive emotions.

But many respected scientists and psychologists are conducting research on positive emotions, and leading this field of research is Barbara Lee Fredrickson, a professor in the Department of Psychology at the University of North Carolina. Her pioneering work into positive emotions is well documented, and she has written two books, published many research articles and made numerous videos, including TED Talks. Some of the outcomes I listed earlier in this chapter have been documented by Fredrickson.

POSITIVE EMOTIONS OFTEN PROVIDE THE FOUNDATION FOR THOSE MEANINGFUL MOMENTS THAT MAKE LIFE WORTH LIVING AND MAKE YOU HAPPY.

———

THE POWER OF
POSITIVE THINKING

It was an obvious choice to finish the book with the theme of positive emotions. Experiencing a range of positive emotions is crucial for effective positive thinking. Positive emotions like joy, hope, inspiration, optimism, love, gratitude, compassion, serenity, happiness and enthusiasm give your life meaning and purpose.

Throughout these 17 chapters I have tried to show you the key themes in thinking positively and how this could enrich your life with new possibilities. Since my stroke 13 years ago, I have discovered why these themes of acceptance, purpose, mindset, optimism, strengths, choices, gratitude, negativity, failure, resilience, values, imagination, dreaming, creativity, goals, identity and positive emotions, have been so important in helping me realize that there is a different, and very rewarding, type of positive thinking that led me to discover so many new possibilities. The introduction to this book is called "My stroke of discovery" because it ultimately led me to having meaning, purpose and happiness in my life. The journey I have been on since I lay in that hospital bed in 2006, unable to communicate with my family and friends, up to the present day, is testament to the type of positive thinking I passionately advocate.

Don't get me wrong, my life is not a utopia! I have days and sometimes weeks where I struggle to find meaning and happiness in what I am doing. I still get stressed, anxious and exhausted. But if I go back and think about some of the themes I explore in this book, and apply some of the ideas I talk about, meaning, purpose and happiness return, and my levels of anxiety and stress reduce. And that is why in the opening sentences of this book I said, "Having a significant stroke at age 41 turned out to be one of the most positive things that has ever happened to me."

As I said in the introduction, the main point of this book was to help rethink positive thinking for the 21st century. The term 'positive thinking' is often associated with the positive thinking movement of the 20th century, which often polarized people. For some, this movement has had significant benefits, while others have found the promise of a better life fundamentally flawed and not based on any proven scientific evidence.

However, having taken the time to read this book, you will by now understand that I am putting forward a fresh, 21st century view of positive thinking that I hope has challenged, inspired and motivated you and will help you to create a world full of possibilities.

REFERENCES
AND RESOURCES

INTRODUCTION

Napoleon Hill, *Think and Grow Rich*, The Ralston Society, 1937.

Norman Vincent Peale, *The Power of Positive Thinking*, Prentice Hall Inc., 1952.

Rhonda Byrne, *The Secret*, Atria Books/Beyond Words, 2006.

Napoleon Hill and W. Clement Stone, *Success Through a Positive Mental Attitude*, Gallery Books, reprint edition, 2007.

Susan David, *Emotional Agility: Get Unstuck, Embrace Change, and Thrive in Work and Life*, Avery, 2016.

Gabriele Oettingen, *Rethinking Positive Thinking: Inside the New Science of Motivation*, Current, 2014.

Martin Seligman, Positive Psychology Center at the University of Pennsylvania, available at: https://ppc.sas.upenn.edu/.

CHAPTER 1   ACCEPTANCE

Fergal Keane, *All of These People*, HarperCollins, 2005.

CHAPTER 2   PURPOSE

Together In Sport, available at: www.togetherinsportrwanda.org.

Dan Buettner, "How to Live to Be 100+," TED Talk, September 2009, available at: https://bit.ly/1o8W3qv.

CHAPTER 3   MINDSET

Bill Gates, *Business @ the Speed of Thought: Succeeding in the Digital Economy*, Grand Central Publishing, 1999.

Bill Gates, *The Road Ahead*, Viking, 1995.

Bill Gates, "The Internet tidal wave," memo, 26 May 1995, available at: https://bit.ly/1CUujZJ.

Carol Dweck, *Mindset: The New Psychology of Success*, Ballantine Books, updated edition, 2007.

Bill Gates, "What you believe affects what you achieve," Gates Notes blog, 7 December 2015, available at: https://bit.ly/1YjkggB.

CHAPTER 4   OPTIMISM

Sam Wong, "Always look on the bright side of life…," *The Guardian*, 11 August 2009, available at: https://bit.ly/2QU2sGS.

Martin Seligman, "Who is Martin Seligman and what does he do?" Positive Psychology Program, 13 March 2017, available at: https://bit.ly/2dj8phU.

Optimism image: by Fotolia/Rafal Olechowski.

Martin Seligman, *Learned Optimism: How to Change Your Mind and Your Life*, Vintage Books USA, 2006.

Learned Optimism Test, available at: https://stanford.io/2cS9BFW.

Learned Optimism Wikipedia, available at: https://bit.ly/2VmPbO0.

CHAPTER 5   STRENGTHS

Gallup StrengthsFinder (now CliftonStrengths), available at: www.gallupstrengthcenter.com.

VIA Character Strengths, available at: www.viacharacter.org.

Sally Bibbs, *The Strengths Book*, LID Publishing, 2017.

Tom Rath and Gallup, *StrengthsFinder 2.0*, Gallup Press, 2007.

CHAPTER 6   CHOICES

Michael Johnson, " 'Olympic mindset' helped recovery from stroke," BBC Sport, 19 November 2018, available at: https://bbc.in/2RZhlsg.

Cyndi Crother, *Catch! A Fishmonger's Guide to Greatness*, Berrett-Koehler, 2005.

Barry Schwartz, "The paradox of choice," TEDGlobal, July 2005, available at: https://bit.ly/1Qcao0e.

Barry Schwartz ''The tyranny of choice," Scientific American, April 2004, available at: https://bit.ly/2zvQ0bg.

CHAPTER 7   GRATITUDE

Robert Emmons "Why Gratitude is Good," Greater Good Science Centre at UC Berkeley at: https://bit.ly/2zS0sro.

David Steindl-Rast, "Want to be happy? Be grateful," TEDGlobal, June 2013, available at: https://bit.ly/1m5MRCo.

CHAPTER 8   NEGATIVITY

Bruce Springsteen, *Born to Run*, Simon & Schuster UK, 2016.

Nick Rufford, "The Boss: Dad couldn't stand me," *Sunday Times*, 25 September 2016, available at: https://bit.ly/2CtHE3F.

CHAPTER 9   FAILURE

Steve Jobs, "Steve Jobs Stanford commencement speech 2005," YouTube, posted 6 March 2006, available at: https://bit.ly/1iDR0rG.

Failure image: Thinkstock.

J.K. Rowling, "Text of J.K. Rowling's speech," Harvard University, 5 June 2008, available at: https://bit.ly/2wPK3VV.

CHAPTER 10   RESILIENCE

US Army, "Comprehensive soldier and family fitness," Wikipedia, available at: https://bit.ly/2TWYbEf.

American Psychology Association, "The road to resilience," available at: https://bit.ly/2K2Bwmc.

CHAPTER 11   VALUES

International Women's Day website, available at: www.internationalwomensday.com.

The Nelson Mandela Foundation, "Wearing Mandela's values," 4 July 2018, available at: https://bit.ly/2FSavms.

CHAPTER 12   IMAGINATION

Malcolm Gladwell, *Outliers: The Story of Success*, Back Bay Books, 2011.

CHAPTER 13   DREAMING

Sean O'Grady, "Martin Luther King's 'I have a dream' speech the greatest oration of all time," *The Independent*, 3 April 2018, available at: https://ind.pn/2RXu16u.

Dr Martin Luther King Jr, "I have a dream," 28 August 1963, YouTube, available at: https://bit.ly/2FBns0G, or read the transcript at: https://bit.ly/2qRkbny.

CHAPTER 14   CREATIVITY

Brandon Stanton, *Humans of New York*, St. Martin's Press, 2015.

CHAPTER 15   GOALS

Ed Stafford, available at: www.edstafford.org.

CHAPTER 16   IDENTITY

Rachel Woods, "Let's rethink ability and autism," TEDx Talk, YouTube, posted, 13 June 2018, available at: https://bit.ly/2tkDRlm.

Jean-Dominique Bauby, *The Diving-Bell and the Butterfly*, HarperCollins, 2008.

CHAPTER 17   EMOTIONS

Kat Lay, "Why positive thinking is the best way to get a grip," *The Times*, 8 January 2019, available at: https://bit.ly/2TAJZkh.

University College London, "Meaningful life tied to healthy ageing", *UCL News*, 7 January 2019, available at: https://bit.ly/2TpX3NX.

Barbara Lee Fredrickson, "Barbara Fredrickson," Wikipedia, available at: https://bit.ly/2VUyhlw.

ABOUT
THE AUTHOR

Neil Francis is the author of *The Entrepreneur's Book* and *Changing Course*. He is currently the chairman of a digital agency, director of one internet company, director of a consultancy practice and a trustee of a social enterprise. At the age of 41, he suffered a stroke that led him to discover a new, meaningful and rewarding life, which led Neil to publish three books and work with many inspiring CEOs, leaders, charity bosses and entrepreneurs.

www.neil-francis.com
neil@neil-francis.com

ABOUT
THE BOOK

Traditionally, the positive thinking philosophy that has permeated Western society advocates that you will achieve whatever you want purely by thinking positive thoughts. On the contrary, at its best, this practice results in success for some individuals, but overall, for the majority it does not!

This book rethinks the true meaning of positive thinking for the 21st century and show that there is more to it than we know. The essence of this book is to demonstrate how a new type of positive thinking can open yourself up to new possibilities. It is then up to each individual to decide which possibilities are achievable and realistic and therefore worth pursuing. *Positive Thinking* explores the ways of creating new possibilities so that you make the right decisions to live a more balanced, meaningful and contented life.